New Budget Landscaping

Other books by Carlton B. Lees

Budget Landscaping

Gardens, Plants, and Man

New Budget Landscaping

Carlton B. Lees

Illustrated by Alexander R. Berry

Holt, Rinehart and Winston   New York

Published by Holt, Rinehart and Winston, 383 Madison Avenue,
New York, New York 10017.

Published simultaneously in Canada by Holt, Rinehart and
Winston of Canada, Limited.

Library of Congress Cataloging in Publication Data
Lees, Carlton B
New budget landscaping.
Includes index.
1. Landscape gardening.   2.   Landscape architecture.
I.   Title.
SB473.L43   712'.6   78-10546
ISBN Hardbound: 0-03-016851-1
ISBN Paperback: 0-03-016846-5

First Edition

Designer: *Susan Mitchell*

Printed in the United States of America

1 3 5 7 9 10 8 6 4 2

Who loves a garden still his Eden keeps.

Amos Bronson Alcott
Tablets, 1868

Contents

Foreword

This book and its antecedent, *Budget Landscaping,* were not written to be the alpha and omega of garden design or landscape organization. They were written to help frustrated homeowners cope with baffling and unused backyards by coming to understand them as three-dimensional, people-containing spaces and by providing a grid system upon which many diverse elements could be organized. For people with considerable design talent, the grid can serve as a jumping-off place, and it may disappear or become absorbed as the garden develops. For others the grid can stand as a strong, simple, and obvious statement of landscape organization. In both cases, however, the hodgepodge typical of many suburban properties is avoided. Usefulness, comfort, pleasure, and value are added. The difference may well be what makes a *home* out of a mere *house.*

The title *Budget Landscaping* had its origin in the concept that through careful planning a homeowner could budget not only his money but also his time and do-it-yourself energy over however long a period proved necessary to complete the job. Such planning ensures that the final outcome makes sense and meets the many needs set down in the beginning.

If good professional help were available to most homeowners, a book such as this one would not have to be written. Unfortunately, relatively few homeowners have a chance to work with architects, much less landscape architects. Most landscape architects do not become involved in small-scale projects. Their attention (and bread and butter) is in larger-scale undertakings such as recreational sites, industrial parks, or shopping centers. There are a few good landscape architects, however, who will work on a consulting basis for an hourly or flat fee. If you can find such an individual, it would be wise to partake of his services as your budget allows.

Many nurserymen and other retailers offer

landscape-design services. Be careful. Many of them are really salesmen working on a commission basis—their job is to sell plants. Of course there are some talented nurserymen who have a clear sense of landscape organization, but by and large they are not well grounded in the principles of design. Also beware of the local lawn-and-yard servicemen who claim to be landscape gardeners. They are usually maintenance people, not landscape gardeners. And do be alert to the decorator types who (usually for a very stiff fee) will fill your yard with an abundance of flowery vegetation and *objets d'art* but provide little in the way of structural and functional design.

Most important, don't accept anyone else's design before spending some time and energy of your own to make sure that it really does what you want.

Building a garden is an exciting experience in which family and friends can become involved. A really good garden contains something of the spirit and personality of those who have created it. It need not be an immaculate high-fashion plate or a multicolored bower. It should be straightforward and honestly yours. Build a garden to please your senses—to see, to smell, to hear, to touch, and to taste—for as many days of each year as possible. Build a garden for yourself.

New Budget Landscaping

1 · In the Beginning

Man was born into a natural environment. He lived intimately with grasses and trees, with the other animals, and with sun, rain, wind, lightning, and the changing seasons. Through his own observations and ingenuity, he found ways to adapt natural phenomena for his own use and pleasure. It was a process of continuing compromise. *Homo sapiens* did not always dominate the natural world; man was but one part of the total, complex fabric.

Although in the earlier stages of his existence man spent much time roaming—perhaps somewhat aimlessly, but also according to seasonal variation and nutritional needs—eventually he came to feel the need for a home from which he could venture forth and return at will. One can also assume that he selected the site for that home with considerable care. Did it offer protection from cold winds, summer sun? Was it high enough to be free from floods in rainy seasons, yet also near a water supply? Was it secluded enough to afford an escape from potential danger, yet open enough to permit him to observe the approach of an enemy or of an animal that could serve as food? A cave, an overhanging cliff, a sheltering boulder, a thicket, the canopy of a great tree—any of these might have served as homesites.

Once the site was selected, how did man change and adapt it to better meet his needs—by gathering a supply of rocks that could be used as weapons, by adjusting the branches of a thicket to create enclosure and camouflage, or by making a hollow in the ground to store food? Whatever he did, the site took on new characteristics: it became a "made place." And while this place may have served as a temporary base at first, as time passed, man became less nomadic and the home more permanent.

When man organized that first bit of landscape,

when he shaped that first place, he created the first garden. Garden is outdoor space organized for man's use, comfort, and pleasure.

It is essential for us to understand this historical relationship between garden and natural world so that we can feel comfortable with nature and manipulate it intelligently. All front yards and backyards, streetscapes, planned subdivisions, and city parks and plazas have their origin in that first bit of landscape man shaped for himself.

If we search through the history and evolution of words we find additional evidence for this: the words *yard, orchard, hortus, garden,* and *paradise* all have a common origin related to the concept of an enclosed, useful, and pleasant place. The word *yard,* for instance, stems from the Middle English *yerd* and the Old English *geard,* meaning enclosure. (In Dutch *gard* means garden.) Similarly the word *orchard* comes from the Middle English *ortgerd* and the Old English *ortigeard.* In the medieval garden, the orchard was the part containing a grove of trees that provided a cool, leafy, and shady shelter, and had nothing to do with the production of apples. The medieval garden and orchard was an important trysting place for knights and their ladies. If only the modern-day *backyard* would follow in the traditions of its predecessors, it could be a much more productive space and it would no longer be necessary to spend as much time and energy seeking seemingly idyllic environments away from home.

It is important to distinguish between places that occur naturally and those that are the result of manipulation by man. Gardening is the most comprehensive of arts, for it encompasses and brings together so many other arts. Versailles and Washington, D.C., are planned, created places, the first designed by Le Nôtre, the second by L'Enfant. Conceptually, both are gardens; architecture, sculpture, painting, music, dance, drama, and all other art forms are contained within them.

As for place-making on a smaller scale, consider Hadrian's villa, Mount Vernon, or Disneyland. These, too, are the creations of man. The overall concept in each case is that of a garden. Mount Vernon was planned by George Washington so that its mansion and outbuildings maintain a careful relationship to sweeping lawns, drives, woodlands, vegetable and flower plots, orchards, and vineyards. While everything is extremely pleasing and has aesthetic value, a work-flow chart would reveal just how well the basic functions were organized. Mount Vernon was extremely useful to the Washingtons. It was comfortable for them, and even today, the pleasure of

Mount Vernon is so apparent that one feels better, and maybe is better, for experiencing it.

The word *villa* in its original definition (and Mount Vernon is a villa) was not a house as we think of it today, but simply a made place. Some spaces are completely open, some are completely enclosed. But what of all the spaces between these two extremes? Is an atrium a room without a ceiling, or a garden with walls? Is a porch a room without walls or a garden with a floor and ceiling? And what of colonnades, peristyles, cloisters, patios, courts, stoas, pavilions, porticoes, pergolas, arbors, grottoes, breezeways, conservatories, gazebos, and glass-walled rooms? Are they not something of both outdoors and indoors?

It is unfortunate that most of us are forced to live in boxlike objects called houses. If we could keep in mind that first man shaping his first place, it would help us to deal better with our living space today. Even boxes can be made more interesting and useful if we can at least mentally break through the tight, confining walls and cope with our living space, indoors and out, as a total concept. By so doing, not only can indoor space be made to relate better to outdoor space, it can also be manipulated to expand our vistas, horizons, and daily experiences.

It is unfortunate, too, that so few of us really understand the concepts embodied in the word *garden*. Too often we limit ourselves to petunia beds and vegetable patches. This practice originated when English ships ruled and roamed the seas, gathering spectacular plants from around the world and bringing them home to England's gentle misty island, where practically every plant on earth can be made to thrive. Horticulture—the culture of the space about the house (*hortus*)—became popular. Architects, poets, and philosophers such as Kent, Bacon, Pope, and Walpole no longer made an intellectual exercise out of shaping garden spaces. Instead gardens became places for collections of plants. And while these botanical riches created a new tradition, the concept of a garden as an art form in terms of organized space was to a large extent lost to the idea of a garden as a collection of plants for decoration. While as spectators we may enter a museum gallery, for example, and see only individual objects, their relationship to each other also creates a composition within the space of the gallery and contributes to our response, whether or not we are aware of it. So it is with a garden—collections of bushes, beans, and begonias do not in themselves make gardens.

The change in the traditional meaning of the word

garden has created a split between the collector horticulturists and the landscape architects (a newly coined term for the most ancient of artisans). Of course there are hacks on both sides, but there are also inspired individuals who understand how to select, shape, and place trees and other plants, materials, and objects within a space.

Gardens in America have suffered too long, not only from this lack of communication between the architect and the plantsman, but also because ecologists, biologists, conservationists, and other disciples of the natural world have remained uninvolved in the shaping of our domestic landscapes. Ironically, speculative builders have had the greatest influence on shaping urban and suburban America. Farms have modified the landscape less disastrously, because they are closely linked to natural phenomena. Farms are conceptually villalike, and even taking into account the misuse and overuse of pesticides, herbicides, chemical fertilizers, and cultivation techniques, farmscapes are still happier, more human environments than are regimented suburban developments and rigid cityscapes.

We have defined *garden* as outdoor space organized for use, comfort, and pleasure. Let's now examine in detail other basic definitions related to shaping landscapes.

First consider the words *area* and *space.* These are often used interchangeably by architects, builders, and interior designers who, perhaps because they usually work with plans on paper, fall into the trap of referring to dining area, living area, or kitchen area. The word *space* has become further confused in recent years with the advent of the term *outer space,* that space beyond the earth's atmosphere.

The words *area* and *space* represent two different ideas. A painting, a wall, a rug, a piece of paper: these have length and width *or* height; they are essentially planes. It is correct to speak of wall area, floor area, or the area of a painting. Space, on the other hand, is three-dimensional. A room, a box, a bottle: these have length, width, *and* height. They are containers. We walk on the area of the floor but we move within the space of the room. It is essential to understand the distinction in order to deal intelligently with indoor and outdoor living spaces, to organize a landscape or shape a garden.

James Rose, a landscape architect, has said that being inside a garden should be like being inside a piece of hollow sculpture. (Imagine being inside one of those huge, free-form Henry Moore nudes!) When inside an architectural sculpture, with its space-capturing beams, cables, and rods, you discover that the artist has not only created an object but has also given shape to space. The feelings you experience when inside a great building are in response to the shape of the enclosed space; the details of the structure are secondary to the quality of that space. If this seems obscure, think of your first reaction to entering a vaulted cathedral, domed capitol, or trussed airplane hangar.

Marjorie Sedgwick, a gardener and friend from north of Boston, refers to "carving out" a garden—she places herself inside a chunk of space and shapes it from within. When her woodsy garden becomes too dense and overgrown, she removes branches to reveal space. Where a sculptor may work with hammer and chisel from within, Mrs. Sedgwick works with a pruning saw from within.

To understand this hollow-sculpture concept—with ourselves as sculptors inside the composition—is to take the first significant step toward dealing with landscapes. In cases such as Mrs. Sedgwick's, where we are already involved with relatively enclosed space, carving-out is the proper approach. In other cases, such as with unbroken prairie space, it becomes necessary to provide definition by placing objects within the space. Remember, the moment the museum curator places an object in an empty gallery, he alters the shape of the space.

We are manipulators of space that already exists. The space within a living room, for example, has always been there. It may once have been a chunk of forest or prairie space that someone enclosed with floor, walls, and ceiling so that temperature could be controlled and rain and mosquitoes kept out. The object was to make the space more useful and pleasurable. If the house is torn down, the space of the room will continue to exist; it merely loses its definition or shape.

To create a garden is to shape outdoor space. The materials we use outdoors—trees, shrubs, hedges, climbing plants, groundcovers—are constantly changing and therefore more interesting to work with than the wood,

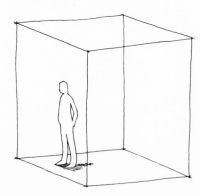

Figure 1

plaster, stone, steel, and textiles used to define indoor space.

Now consider the word *organization*. I once worked on a large exhibit of acacias that included about a hundred tubbed or potted trees and shrubs of various heights and shapes. As the exhibit neared completion, a young member of my staff exclaimed, "My God, if that isn't making order out of chaos, I don't know what is!" Without realizing it, he had defined the design process. He had seen the plants placed helter-skelter as they were unloaded from a huge van, and he had observed the process of moving each plant into its place, bringing

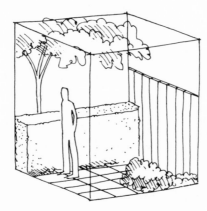

Figure 2

other kinds of plants with different shapes and colors into the scheme, and then placing benches where visitors could sit under the overhanging yellow-flowered branches. He had observed the making of a garden to serve as a useful entryway, which was also a comfortable place to move through and a pleasant space to experience. The entire scheme had more than just a decorative purpose, since it provided introduction and direction for the 100,000 people who saw the show.

With so much of what is currently produced for commercial consumption concerned more with decoration than function, the word *design* has lost clear definition. As a result, honest beauty is often lost. A brown egg has beauty; a sequin-studded deodorant container for the bathroom does not. Understanding the difference is essential if we are not to be impressed with plastic daisies and spawn them where real daisies once grew.

Design is organization, nothing more. This is not to say that it is easy. Indeed it is a complex process which must take into consideration many factors, both obvious and subtle, and its success depends upon the skill with which these factors are organized. And while beauty is usually a desired result, it should not be the primary one. If we try to create beauty without a more fundamental purpose, the result may be merely pretty.

Along with our definition of garden, consider the words *use, comfort,* and *pleasure.* I sometimes feel that Mr. and Mrs. Split-level/Ranch-house/Garrison/Cape/Contemporary America think of landscape only in terms of what their house looks like to everyone who drives by, and no more. This is reminiscent of nineteenth-century Wild West America, where saloons, general stores, and sheriffs' offices had streetside facades bigger and more glorious than the buildings behind them. From such a past we have been influenced to design houses more to be seen than to be lived in, houses that rely on superficial decorations such as tacked-on porticoes, bastard mansard roofs, pictureless picture windows, snap-in snap-out plastic mullions (your choice—Elizabethan diamonds or Georgian rectangles), and mustache foundation plantings.

The three words *use, comfort,* and *pleasure* put the emphasis precisely where it should be, and in the proper order. If we apply them to the approach to the front door, for example, the word *use* determines that it should be direct, unimpeded, and take us from where we are to where we want to go. *Comfort* requires that it should be wide, firm, smooth, and easy to travel. And *pleasure* establishes that both the arrangement and the material used should be good-looking. Pleasure is not just visual,

of course, for it also relates to comfort and usefulness. Getting to the front door should not be a boring or burdensome trip, but rather an interesting experience for you, for members of your family, for your guests, and for all others who have occasion to come to your door.

Whether you are organizing a room or a garden, organize for your *own* use, comfort, and pleasure. Don't worry about what others think, or about style. Anyone can have department-store decor or catalog landscaping. You have a right to something better.

We are, after all, concerning ourselves with our environment. Ecology begins at home. Most of us acknowledge this, and we expend a considerable amount of time, effort, and money to make our indoor spaces useful, comfortable, and pleasurable. Most of us are concerned about outdoor spaces but are baffled by them. This is understandable, since outdoor space is more difficult to define or measure than a room indoors. And the outdoors changes: shrubs grow, leaves change color, trees support heavy masses of foliage in summer but become a tracery of lines in winter. Tulips bloom, then disappear; evergreens are more spectacular in a glittery, snowy landscape than amid lush summer greenery. But these very complexities provide the garden-maker with excitement and richness that no painter can ever possess on his palette, no sculptor can find in a quarry, and no interior designer can develop with wood, paper, textile, or paint.

By taking advantage of outdoor space—by organizing it for use, comfort, and pleasure—we can add immeasurably to the quality of our lives. And what we do with our own chunk of landscape space contributes to our neighborhood, to our town, and to the quality of the total landscape. The result is a better environment for everyone.

2 · Spaces and Materials

The plot of land we call home is the floor of the space in which we live. Although its contour, texture, and color may vary, the land is simply the bottom inside surface of a volume of space. Some of this surface has been used as a base for the house, which itself subdivides the volume to create indoor spaces.

Indoor living space divides easily into four categories: public access, general living, private living, and work space. Although these categories are less absolute outdoors than inside, they still exist, often as extensions of indoor space. A porch, terrace, or patio is an extension of the living room, dining room, or family room. The front yard is an extension of the entry hall.

Public Access Space

Public access space provides a transition between the street and the living spaces within a house. Indoors, the public access space might be an entry hall or, if there is no formal hall, any space that serves the same purpose. Outside the front door, the public access space may be partly defined by an entrance porch, portico, canopy, or stoop, and extends to the public street or roadway. It may contain or be defined by a walkway, paving, driveway, or parking site. Foliage from trees and shrubs create visual barriers and overhead canopies, providing enclosure. The house facade also helps define this space. Distant hills, neighboring houses, utility poles—anything you see or experience as you pass through the public access space from the street to the house—becomes part of that space. To a lesser extent, public access space includes the back or service door and the space on either side of it where deliveries, handymen, or young children fresh from a sandbox or snowbank are received. Public access space often overlaps with a kitchen or carport, spaces that serve more than one function. It also affects the view from all adjacent indoor and outdoor spaces.

Try to visualize a volume that has no particular size or shape but extends from inside your front door outward into the landscape. Think of the free-form shapes you or your children may have made when kneading bread dough or clay. Imagining the inside of these shapes will help you to comprehend landscape volume. Public access space—indeed all space—can flow in the manner of a Henry Moore sculpture, which contains holes and tunnels that connect with other spaces associated with the same or similar functions. If you can place people inside these spaces, study their movements, and retain a vision of their paths (much like nighttime photographs of the lights of moving automobiles), you will understand James Rose's definition of gardens as "hollow sculpture."

General Living Space

Indoors, all members of the household share certain spaces, such as the living room, library, or family room. The kitchen is also fast becoming as much of a social center as it is a work space. Outdoor living space func- s in the same manner as its indoor counterpart, ex- that it also provides an escape from confining walls. f outdoor living space is to be useful, comfortable,

and pleasurable, at least a moderate degree of privacy is required. Thus a portion of the property away from the street and distinctly separate from public access space should be devoted to family activity and entertaining. This is the much abused or underused backyard. Your backyard is a potential gold mine. Don't waste it.

An uninterrupted flow from indoor general living space to the outdoors promotes efficient linking of indoor and outdoor functions. (An outdoor dining space, for example, should be organized in the same manner as a formal indoor dining room, recognizing two basic needs: gracious access for family and guests, and easy access to the kitchen.) A porch—open, screened, or even glazed in the winter to become a plant room—may serve as a transitional space between indoors and outdoors, with some characteristics of both, and can also be used as general living space, as can many transitional spaces. The New Orleans patio, a direct descendant of the Roman atrium (a roofless central court that may also serve as an entryway), is another wonderful transitional space. The term *patio* has been used in America to define any paved place outdoors only since about 1950. Before that, the term *terrace* was used to designate such places, especially in the Northeast. But that word is no more correct than *patio*, unless of course this paved portion was elevated and provided overlook as well as easy access from indoors. A large paved area or deck is an excellent place for family and friends to gather outdoors.

Garden or plant rooms are a recent development. They are transitional spaces that enable homeowners to include growing plants in their environments all year long. Some, like greenhouses, are built with commercially available components, others are custom-designed and very sophisticated, and some rely on do-it-yourself ingenuity. Dining-room, bedroom, bathroom, and kitchen spaces can be extended, opened up, or glazed to allow light in and capture the essence of the outdoors. These garden or plant rooms provide physical as well as seasonal passage. They emphasize our need for constant contact with the natural world and allow us to maintain some of the fragrance and vitality of summer throughout the year. The impact of this exciting development can be seen in the recently built shopping malls and corporate structures that include glass-enclosed gardens. While we may think of such developments as innovative, in many ways they represent a return to that wonder of wonders, the Victorian conservatory, which was the setting for intimate gatherings as well as great parties, a hideaway for young lovers, and a place of mystery for small children.

Uniting indoor and outdoor space is much easier when there are transitional places, yet builders have made very little effort to provide for them. Direct access from the living room or other rooms in a house to a private garden is an ancient nicety that has been omitted from most modern American box-houses. Indeed, many suburban development homes have no rear door of any kind. This dilemma can be avoided simply by installing sliding glass doors instead of a restrictive window at the back of the house. This situation has been changing slightly as some mass builders begin to utilize concepts architects and custom builders have been using for years.

Private Living Space

Private indoor living space provides sleeping and bathing accommodations for the family. How is it related to the outdoors? As much as it is necessary to close windows, pull shades, or draw draperies because of noises, lights, hot sun, smells, dust, or other outside influences, there are also times when we benefit from bringing a little outdoors inside. The Romans reaped much pleasure from turning their baths into gardens, and today the bathroom is still the indoor space most in need of being drenched with sunlight and fresh air and filled with plants.

Sliding glass doors leading to a small deck or terrace facing east off your bedroom can make getting up in the morning much easier. In warm weather, stepping directly outdoors after awakening, especially if a swimming pool is close by, can be exhilarating. A terrace also affords a wonderful proximity to moonlight, flower fragrances, bird songs, and the sound of rain. Even in winter, though the temperature may not be inviting, the glass doors and terrace provide an immediate view of the outdoors and its weather.

Work Space

Work space indoors includes the strictly functional part of the kitchen, the food-storage and laundry spaces, and may flow outdoors to include a clothesline, trash containers, or a stack of wood for the fireplace. It includes the garage and the open space adjacent to it. Work space is not always as clearly recognizable as public access or general living space, because it may be temporary or integrated with other spaces. A clothesline or collapsible clothes reel can be erected in a general living space when

needed and stored at other times. A greenhouse is a space for both work and pleasure. A garden toolshed, cold frames, or compost bins can be established adjacent to one another or where most needed within the garden space.

Ideally, the service door, garage or carport, and basement entranceway should all be in one place, so that odd bits of lumber, tools, toys, and those objects that are too good to throw away can be stored and retrieved with a minimum of steps.

Establishing Your Point of View

Having analyzed how space functions indoors and out, we must now establish our position within those spaces. The hollow-sculpture concept requires that we place ourselves firmly within the composition and organize the space around us. Your landscape includes anything that can be seen from a given point at a given moment—the land and all the objects on it, both natural and man-made, the soil, grass, trees, rocks, water, even the sky.

Colors, textures, and landscape composition may change from season to season. Imagine standing in the middle of a hillside cornfield in June. The view would be very broad indeed, especially if the hill happened to overlook an expanse of countryside. Now visualize standing on the same spot in the middle of August, when the corn is 8 feet tall. The landscape would be reduced to a pattern of interweaving cornstalks, leaves, and tassels, and a few glimpses of the sky above and the earth below.

Beginning with the backyard, look at your own landscape. Notice that in summer, when trees, shrubs, and herbaceous plants are heavy with foliage, your vistas are quite different than in winter, when the leaves are down and you can see beyond trees and shrubs to a rock or subtle earth contour that was concealed by a flowering summer plant. Your landscape changes not only in color and texture but also in size and illusion of size. Even in a completely confined city backyard, the canopy of a tree or vine can alter or appear to alter the size or shape of the space as the seasons change.

When organizing landscape space, we must think of "concentric balance" instead of the "symmetrical/ asymmetrical balance" of the picture-perfect landscape. The pictoral approach requires us to stand still in space—which we rarely do. The concentric viewpoint allows us to deal with landscape space as it surrounds us and as we move through it. Imagine yourself as the core of a sphere. Radiating lines extend from you in all direc-

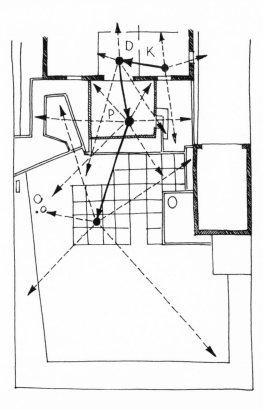

Figure 3 · As we move from kitchen to dining room to screened porch to garden, our lines of movement (solid) and of sight (broken) change.

tions to every object you can see, touch, smell, hear, or taste at a given moment. These experience lines ("lines of sight," if for the sake of simplicity we limit ourselves to vision) are not all of uniform length because, unlike a sphere, a garden is not a symmetrical container. Change positions; note how much the landscape has changed in its relationship to you. Indoors, objects are placed in relationship to how we move through a room. Approaching the organization of backyard, front yard, and other parts of the landscape in the same manner as we would the more familiar territory of a living room ensures that the result is a useful, comfortable, and pleasurable garden and not a scattering of unrelated landscape features. It also reinforces our awareness of what already exists and can be used to best advantage.

Stand in your backyard, in one spot, and look up, down, and outward as you slowly pivot 360 degrees. What do you see? Grass, ivy, flagstone, petunias, gravel, sky, an arbor, overhanging branches, the wall of your house, a cluster of lilacs, a hedgerow, a tall neighboring building, a distant pine, and the sky meeting the edge of a far hill. Perhaps you can also see a trash can, a compost heap, and a sagging fence. Beyond what you see, what about what you hear and smell? These too are part of the landscape.

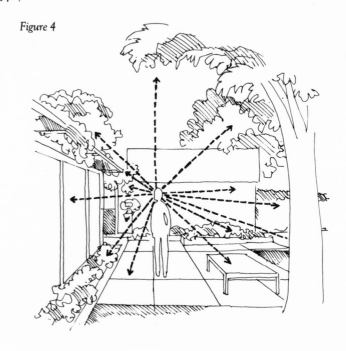

Figure 4

Now that we have considered space as hollow sculpture, have analyzed it in terms of function related to our needs, and have established our position within it, we must also understand the concepts of floor, wall, and ceiling, as they apply to outdoor space, before we can manipulate it successfully.

Garden Floor

The garden floor is anything that covers the bottom inside of the landscape space. It is basically the land itself, but may have many variations in form, texture, color, and material. Lawn is the basic component of the garden floor. Although we may complain about mowing and feeding it, lawn is the easiest to maintain, least expensive, coolest, and generally most comfortable of all garden floors. In terms of design, lawn is often misused as whatever is left after the trees and flower beds have been planted. But lawn can have a clean, interesting, and exciting shape of its own; this is the key to a good garden floor. Even in the North, the basic lawn grasses are green all winter—maybe not as brilliant as in June, but green nonetheless.

Lawn consists of countless living grass plants. Since a garden's basic purpose is to provide contact with the natural world, it is prudent to consider this wonderful green carpet as our number-one choice for flooring material. If your property is large enough, you might use meadow grasses and wildflowers, which need be mowed only once a year (in autumn, after frost has occurred and the seed has ripened to ensure continuity), and through which you could maintain frequently mowed paths to create inviting and comfortable walkways.

In places exposed to heavy foot traffic, where dry and firm footing is needed for chairs, benches, tables, and other furniture, or where extensive tree roots absorb nutrients and water that the grass needs, it is necessary to use materials such as stone, brick, concrete, gravel, wood blocks, or shade-tolerant plants on the garden floor.

In woodsy places, the landscape floor may be covered with the mulch of decaying leaves and twigs mixed with mosses, ferns, and other small, shade-tolerant plants. In more formal gardens, the floor may be covered with plants such as vinca, ivy, pachysandra, or with a mulch

Figure 5

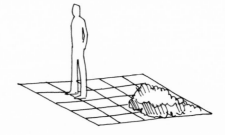

of fir bark, peat moss, or pebbles arranged in neat patterns. Ground cover can also be of crushed stone, crushed clam or oyster shells (if you live near the ocean), wood chips, pine needles, sawdust, or tanbark. Fine-particled gravel, sand, clay, and soil, kept tamped and rolled or neatly raked or swept as in Japanese gardens, also make good garden floors. Mulches of crushed brick, fine coal, and coarse sand are very much a part of elaborate French gardens. Panels of lawn can be defined by bands of bare earth, turning the panels into great green carpets on the ground.

Beds of flowering plants can also be floor covers. Plantings of flowering and foliage plants in low, intricate patterns (carpet bedding) simulate decorative carpets on the garden floor. *Parterre*, meaning "on the ground," is the proper term for the elaborate ground patterns of the Italian and French Renaissance gardens. Ponds and pools of water as a part of the garden floor allow us to look down into them or enjoy reflections of sky and branches overhead.

Wood decks, previously mentioned as transitional devices, are particularly useful on uneven terrain, where they can be built to project outward and emphasize a distant view. They can also be used on flat land, where they are best placed a step or two above ground level in order to promote air movement and drainage and to prevent rotting. Prefabricated deck sections are available in many lumberyards and can be picked up and moved to another part of the yard or to a new property, hence are practical if yours is a rented house.

The garden floor combines many elements to create the basic ground pattern that holds the garden together. As you begin to plan your garden floor, think of it as a giant bas-relief. Your drawing need not be expertly rendered, but it should reveal good basic design. The importance of a well-defined floor plan cannot be overemphasized. Remember as you study garden plans and develop your own that the plants growing out of the floor are soft, irregular in shape, complex in texture, and constantly changing. The stability of the basic floor pattern is absolutely necessary to hold together all the other variables in the garden.

Garden Wall

The garden wall is whatever terminates our horizontal vision. While we are always in close physical contact with the garden floor, our relationship to the garden walls changes as we change position, in more ways than just our distance from them—for example, a 3-foot hedge is a garden wall only when we are seated.

In his book *Landscape for Living*, Garrett Eckbo emphasizes the importance of garden walls when he defines gardens as "outdoor space around private homes, sufficiently enclosed or isolated for the private use of the individual families." Obviously, garden walls may vary from hard architectural structures to distant vistas of hills, prairie, ocean, or horizon. Between these extremes are countless variations: hedges, fences, shrub masses, tree trunks, low-branched flowering trees, houses, garages, barns, wooded hillsides, or pastures with grazing cows. Like garden floors, garden walls also change colors and textures. A shrub mass may be leafless in winter, alive with new leaves in spring, clothed with flowers in early summer, and covered with brilliant orange-red fruits and bronze-purple foliage in autumn. A hedgerow can provide a visual barrier, screening out unwanted views or keeping nosy neighbors at bay, while itself being an object of beauty.

A hedge of fiery red or intense rose-purple azaleas can be wonderful, depending on how, when, and where it is used and its relationship to the overall garden structure. Color need not be used sparingly, but it should be compatible with your overall design, not a spectacular hodgepodge. And remember, substantial, seemingly subtle, and less colorful flowers or foliages can provide richer, longer-lasting effects if enough thought and care are given to placement.

Creation of garden walls affords much flexibility. If you want to develop privacy for a house close to another house or a street, you'll need a wall at least six feet high. When selecting the material most appropriate for this barrier, keep in mind its relationship to other structures and materials, available space, maintenance, air movement, sound penetration, costs, and the time you are willing to wait—for a shrub or tree to grow, for instance.

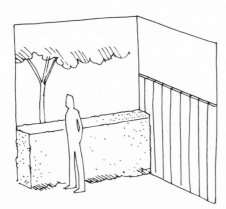

Figure 6

The most expensive solution is to build an actual wall of brick, stone, adobe, cast concrete, or concrete blocks. A stockade fence made of boards, saplings, or bamboo, whether solid, paneled, woven, or louvered (to allow air movement but block vision), would also do the job. The fence might also be constructed from a wood or pipe frame with panels of welded wire (farm fencing), lattice, or netting, or strung with ropes, cables, or wires covered with climbing plants such as grape, honeysuckle, woodbine, bittersweet, or clematis, which could provide a visual barrier while promoting air movement.

Using a hedge—a row of plants of any height, all of one kind, and rigidly sheared, lightly pruned, or left to develop naturally—can provide a less immediate solution to the problem. A sheared evergreen hedge is nearly as architectural as a masonry wall. Since we do not sit outdoors in winter, at least in cool climates, hedges need not be evergreen; summer foliage usually provides all the privacy we need. Hedges require more ground area than a man-made wall or fence. Sheared hedges can usually be confined to a width of three or four feet. Where space allows, shrubs that grow uniformly and maintain lower branches as they mature make excellent hedges that do not have to be sheared. A width of about eight feet is needed for doublefile viburnum, regel privet, or flowering quince, for example. Low-branched flowering trees such as dogwood, fringe tree, or sweet bay can be used as hedges, but of course the width will be much wider than that of a fence or sheared hedge. This exercise in pursuit of privacy reveals how many ways there are to solve the problem by selecting the garden wall which best meets your needs.

Many communities have established specific rules and regulations limiting fence heights to four feet or less. Although some of these ordinances contain the terms *enclosing* and *boundary* and imply structures on property lines, they do not forbid the use of panels or freestanding sections of fence that serve the same purpose as folding screens used as indoor room dividers. The word *fence* implies barrier, but who is to say when a structure stops being a fence and becomes a decorative panel or support for a vine?

Another law that is often misunderstood or misinterpreted is one that requires a swimming pool to be enclosed by a fence. This enclosure does not have to be immediately around the pool, separating it from the rest of the garden, nor does it have to be strictly utilitarian or constructed from one material. As long as children are prevented from wandering onto your property and falling into the pool, the fence can be as imaginative and as much a part of the total garden scheme as you like. It may be entirely visible or it may be completely masked by shrubs, hedges, or vine plantings. Evergreen climbers such as euonymus can be trained to grow through the mesh of some fences and then be sheared like a formal hedge. This completely obscures the fence but meets all legal requirements.

The side walls of garages, barns, and other buildings—including the house—often lend themselves to special treatment, especially when they are viewed in relationship to the garden rather than as mere building walls. Climbing plants can be used to clothe walls and reduce their impact as architectural structures, trees and shrubs can be trained to grow flat as espaliers against a building wall, and climbing plants can be attached with wire to the wall around windows or doors in formal or geometric patterns or in more irregular and natural ways. Lattices are another architectural device that can make a wall more interesting.

Color can be applied to a wall so that it becomes an integral part of the total garden scheme. In one of my own gardens I realized that one wall of my garage was more important to me as part of the garden than as a garage wall. I therefore painted the wall a dark charcoal-gray to provide more dramatic background for the daffodils, lilies, chrysanthemums, and an orange-fruited tea-viburnum shrub in front of it.

Prefabricated fences and similar readily available materials offer quick and easy solutions to some garden problems, but don't limit yourself to these materials "as is." A common stockade fence, for example, can be refined by either sawing off the jagged pointed "teeth" in a straight line and capping the panels with 2-by-4s, or by attaching 1-by-6 or 1-by-8 boards on each side of the fence panel so that the top edge of the boards is even with the tips of the teeth, then capping the vertical elements with another board. Either procedure will create a finish similar to the coping on a masonry wall. Treat the addition with clear wood preservative. Sunlight shining on the clear preservative seems to hasten the natural weathering process, and within a year the wood will become a pleasant silvery-gray.

Most of the plants used to create garden walls are either medium- or large-sized shrubs or small trees, although some smaller shrubs are appropriate in some situations—such as where you want to see over the wall when you are standing but not when you're seated, or where an elevated contour helps provide necessary privacy.

Garden Ceiling

If someone asked you what you see when you look upward when outside, you might think the only logical answer would be sky. But don't forget that the sky varies in color and mood depending on the weather and time of day. Tree canopies—rugged white oak, romantic weeping willow, elegant elms, sugar and red maples with pewter-colored bark in late winter and blazing foliage in autumn—are also part of that garden ceiling. Trees can be the delight of a garden; they are also the dependable anchors upon which spatial organization depends.

Trees capture space. The trunk, branches, and twigs reach upward and interact with space in much the same manner as roots divide and subdivide in the earth. They also create an overhead canopy of shelter and security. Visualize two similar houses, one with and one without a tree canopy. The former is surely more pleasant and welcoming.

Where no trees exist, other devices can function as garden ceiling. Pergolas and arbors have been used throughout history to provide a shade canopy of grapevines and other climbing plants, and have long been favorite sites for weddings and other gatherings.

People are likely to be ill at ease in a situation where they do not sense some enclosure. Although some of us are comfortable in very small enclosed spaces, others feel claustrophobic in such an environment and react better to larger spaces with open vistas and as little confinement as possible. But nearly all of us feel the need for some relief from the vastness of the sky. For this reason a ceiling of some sort is needed if we are to feel complete-

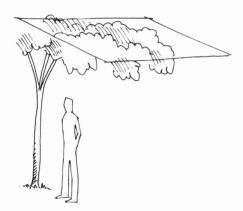

Figure 7

ly comfortable in a garden. Besides, think how much more interesting the sky becomes when seen through grapevines or trees.

Tree canopies also provide natural air conditioning against the sun's oppressive heat and are particularly useful for shielding windows. A dogwood or treelike lilac can be planted as close as 3 or 4 feet from the house, just to one side of a window. This will cause little loss of vision while actually improving the view as seen through the branches of the tree, especially with flowers or leaves changing color. Unlike some man-made awnings, trees do not inhibit air movement. Several small trees (with a mature height of 30 feet or less) create leafy canopies in small gardens, particularly if they are used in a group of three or more. These same plants can also be used to shape a garden wall.

Even after you have chosen the kind of tree suitable for a given situation, the selection of the actual plants is critical. For example, if you want to close out an unwanted view with a hedgerow of dogwoods, select plants with many low side branches. If on the other hand your aim is to create a grove—say, a cluster of three or four dogwoods under which garden furniture can be grouped—it is necessary to select plants having strong vertical growth and few side branches. No matter how young a tree is when you buy it, it is generally fairly easy to determine whether it has strong side branches or a strong vertical leader. To encourage vertical growth, remove low twigs that might otherwise develop into side branches. Pruning vertical leaders will slow vertical growth and create low mass. Pruning, properly practiced, is a very useful art.

The plant selection charts starting on page 134 provide more information on the materials and specific plants that may be used for garden floors, walls, and ceilings.

3 • How to Measure, Record, Define, and Explore

Now that we've established what a garden is and what it's made of, it's time to make a reasonably accurate plan on paper of your property as it now exists. This allows you to study the whole landscape and try various solutions to your problem before arriving at the final one. It is much less expensive, less time-consuming, and easier on the back muscles to work first on paper instead of making the usual beginner's mistakes of planting a tree in a space too small or a 3-foot shrub where a 6-foot one could have given needed privacy. A plan also provides a diagram, a form of shorthand for future reference.

For this stage of landscaping you will need a few things readily available from any store selling drafting supplies. Many of these items may already be tucked away somewhere in your desk.

Paper. Use two or three sheets of 17-by-23-inch graph or cross-section paper, the kind marked off in squares. Be sure it has eight lines to the inch, with every eighth line darker than the others, so that the paper is marked off in ⅛-inch squares by pale lines and in 1-inch squares by darker lines. Since each small square will equal one square foot of ground measurement, a 17-by-23-inch sheet of paper will accommodate property measuring as large as 136 by 184 feet.

Buy the kind of tracing paper used by draftsmen, either bond or vellum. Both come in rolls or pads. Pads, available in various sizes, are easier to use and sufficient for your needs. The 18-by-24-inch size is most compatible with the graph paper you'll be using. The pad's cardboard backing is usually firm enough to provide a rigid base for working outdoors. Eventually, your vellum pad will contain a file of final drawings, all of which can be reproduced inexpensively as blue-line prints by any draftsman's printing service.

For experimental sketches, use inexpensive yellow tracing paper, which comes in 12-inch rolls. Use lots of this to develop ideas before transferring them to the vellum. One roll provides a large supply of this transparent paper, so you can use it freely.

Pencils. For careful drawings, 2H pencils are usually adequate, but buy two or three 3B pencils for sketching or scribbling. If you have never used these very soft pencils, you will be amazed how much easier it is to draw lines with them. They reduce the friction between mind and paper. Colored pencils or nylon-tipped pens are also useful for designating specific items such as view-lines, underground drainage lines, or septic fields on your base plan, each color representing a specific system. (These colors can also be used to identify materials such as paving, lawn, and groundcover when you begin to design on paper.)

Ruler. Use a 12-inch ruler with a good edge for drawing straight lines. If calibrations confuse you, get a ruler with divisions no smaller than ⅛-inch. If you own an architect's scale, you can also use that for measuring lines and will be able to read dimensions directly in feet.

Compass. Compasses are used to draw circles and are available in any five-and-dime store. (If you have children, you probably have several compasses somewhere in your house.)

Drawing Board. Sophisticates may use a regulation drawing board, but a sheet of ⅛-inch tempered masonite from a lumberyard will serve just as well and is less expensive. Furthermore, you can take it outdoors and not have to worry about its getting damp or soiled—treatment to which good drawing boards should not be subjected. Have the tempered masonite cut to the size of your vellum pad (probably 18 by 24 inches), unless your property measures larger than 136 by 184 feet. In that case, tape two sheets of graph paper together, being careful to match the lines. Outline your property on the paper, cut off any excess, and have the masonite board cut to size. If your lot is so large that the drawing board would be unwieldy, fold under part of the paper and work on one section at a time. (You can also make an overall plan of your property at sixteen-scale—16 feet to the inch—and blow up portions to eight-scale as you work on them.)

Paper Clips. Get four large clips, the kind you can open by squeezing the handles together. Use the clips to attach your plan to the drawing board or pad. They are easier to use than drafting tape, especially when you have two or three sheets of tracing paper on the board.

Scale Explained

To get an accurate plan of your landscape as it exists, let each small square of the graph paper represent one square foot. In other words, a line 3 feet long on the lawn will appear only three small squares long on paper. A square of concrete that measures 8 feet on each side will appear on the graph paper as a square having eight of the small squares along each of its edges, and would be an inch long on each side. This is called ⅛- or eighth-scale. To make sure you understand this procedure, quickly answer these questions:

- A line 5 inches long on the paper represents a line how many feet long in the landscape? (40 feet)

- A 14-foot line on the ground will measure how long on paper? (1¾ inches, or 14 small graph-paper squares)

- A line 2½ inches long on paper equals how long a line on the ground? (20 feet)

- A line 6 inches long on the ground is how long on paper? (¹/₁₆ inch, or half of a small graph-paper square)

These questions should help you understand how to work with a reduced scale if you have never done so. Actually, it is not necessary to convert every line measurement into inches—often you can simply count squares, one for each foot of land. This is where the larger squares bounded by the dark lines on the graph paper come in handy. Since there are seven pale lines between each pair of dark ones, the small squares are easily counted off in groups of eight. If you are recording a line 40 feet long on the landscape, you need only count five large squares instead of forty small ones—except, of course, if the line you are measuring runs obliquely to the lines on the paper; then use your ruler.

Read ground measurements to the nearest half foot; accuracy beyond that is unnecessary in most instances. Where a ground measurement reads 3 feet 3 inches, record it as 3½ feet on the plan; if it reads 3 feet 2 inches, record it as 3 feet on the plan. Make a special effort, though, to be as accurate as possible in the plan with sidewalks, drives, fences, and other structural elements.

If you have your house blueprints, they can supply you with helpful dimensions. Even with a tract-built house, it is possible that the builder or developer might have not only a house plan but also a plan (called a plat) showing the position of the house on the site. If so, you are lucky, for you need only convert from the scale of the house plans (usually in ¼- or quarter scale) or from the plat (which may be in ten-, sixteen-, or twenty-scale). Be sure to note the scale so you do not make errors in transferring the information to your own eighth-scale graph paper.

If the scale still seems confusing, ask someone who has had drafting or mechanical-drawing experience to explain it to you.

Measuring Outdoors

The process described below is not technically perfect, but it will provide information accurate enough if your property is a relatively simple one. You will need strong string (mason's twine, available at hardware stores, is ideal), a few foot-long stakes made from scraps of lumber whittled to a point at one end, and a 100-foot measuring tape. Low-cost tapes are available at drafting-supply shops and hardware stores. (If you can borrow a second 100-foot tape, the measuring will be much easier and quicker.) You will also need an assistant, someone to help hold and read the tape.

If your lot is flat and perfectly rectangular, draw in the boundary lines. If your corner markers are nonexist-ent or if you can't find them, put a stake at each corner to serve as a temporary reference point. If your neighbors are sensitive about this sort of thing, err a few inches in their favor. Nothing brings out a neighbor more quickly than a measuring tape on a lot line, and there is no need to cause any agitation at this point—you may really need to be in his or her good graces later on, especially if you plan to erect a fence or plant a hedge along the boundary line. Disputes, of course, can be solved by a licensed surveyor.

If you do not have a developer's plan of the property, transfer the house plan (at correct scale) to the graph paper, locating it by roughly measuring the distance from the street to the house. If you are also without a plan of the house, simply measure all the outside walls and then locate and record all doors, windows, steps, porches, chimney protrusions, etc. Only first-floor features are needed. When measuring, be sure to hold your tape taut and level. While the outside walls are not a foot thick in most houses, for ease in reading your plan, they can be drawn to the thickness of one square on the graph paper. Leave the windows clear, and draw in only the outside line to represent doorways, as shown in Figure 8. The division of interior space need be only approximate enough to show the relationship of the rooms to the outdoors and help you analyze your outdoor views from within the house. Since most corners are square and few odd angles appear in houses, getting a plan down on paper should not be difficult.

To locate the corners of your property accurately on paper, especially if the boundary lines are not parallel to the house walls or if your lot is a very odd shape, use the corners of the house as base points. Measure from each of the base points (A and B in Figure 8) to each of the corners (C and D). Since points A and B are already established on paper, distances A–C and B–C become radii (half the diameters) of two imaginary circles. Open a compass so the distance from the pivot point to the point of the pencil is equal to A–C, and draw an arc using A as the center of the circle, then adjust the compass so the distance between pivot and pencil point equals B–C and draw another arc using B as the center. Point C will fall exactly where these two arcs cross. To locate point D, follow the same procedure, using lines A–D and B–D as the radii for the arcs. Now draw a straight line connecting points C and D. If you have measured carefully and made no mistakes, this line will correspond in length with the distance between the two

points outdoors; more important, it will locate these points and the resulting boundary line in relationship to the house, even if house wall A–B and lot line C–D are far from parallel to each other.

This same system is used for locating the other corners of the lot: point E is located by measuring G–E and H–E, and point F is located by measuring G–F and H–F. Even if you think your lot is perfectly rectangular, it's a good idea to locate the corners on paper in this manner, because angles between the house wall and an invisible lot line may not be apparent to the eye. Any convenient house corners will do for base points as long as you are careful to use their correct counterparts on paper and your house plan is accurate. After lettering the corners on paper, write them on the house wall with a piece of chalk to avoid confusion. The chalk will rub off easily when the mark is no longer needed. As long as you can measure in straight lines, the system just described can be used to find all objects in the landscape.

Where several shrubs have grown together, you can measure the spread of their mass and simply sketch in its approximate position on the plan, since the shrubs are more indefinite in outline than is a tree or architectural object. If possible, however, it is best to indicate points at which stems arise from the ground. Be especially careful, though, when locating trees or other definite objects that are apt to remain in the finished garden. Suppose, for instance, that you had a large shade tree you wanted to include in a paved outdoor sitting area. A measuring error could destroy a design concept.

If the ground is very far from level, measuring in straight lines up or down a slope will not give a true picture of the landscape, since only horizontal dimensions are seen on paper. If you have banks or slopes on your property, you can locate them more accurately on paper by using the following method. You will need mason's twine, tall stakes, and a string or line level, the

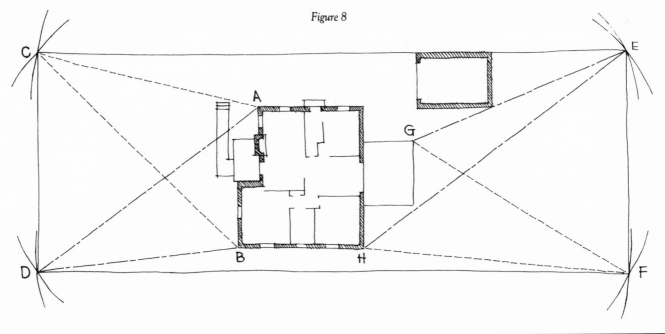

Figure 8

latter being an inexpensive item used by masons and available in hardware stores. You will also need an assistant.

If, as in Figure 9, A represents the corner of the house and E the point to be located (in this case a tree), place a small stake at A and a taller one at a point (C) not more than five feet lower than A, for ease in measuring. Fasten the twine to the stake near ground level (A), and then have your assistant pull tightly while holding it against the stake at C. Hang the string level on the twine about midway between corner A and stake C, and have your assistant raise or lower the twine on the tall stake until the bubble shows the twine to be level. Mark the stake at this point (B), which is level with the ground at the corner of the house. Holding the tape taut, measure A−B. Record the measurement. To find the tree, repeat the twine-and-level process from the bottom of the tall stake (C) to the corresponding level on the tree (D) (or to another stake, if the point you are trying to establish—E—is a corner point). Remember that stake C must be in direct line between the house corner and the tree, and that this whole process must be repeated between another corner of the house and the tree in order to locate it by the two-arc, or triangle, method. If necessary, this step method can be repeated several times to reach your destination.

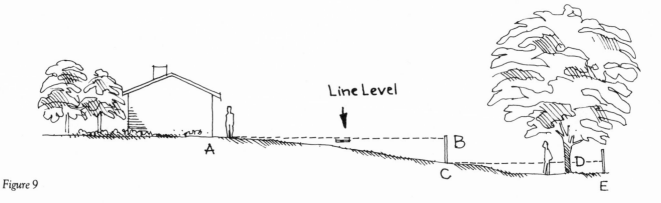

Figure 9

This stake-and-string level system is also used for measuring the slope of a bank. If as in Figure 10 you wish to level the ground near the house and build a terrace from A to B, the distance between B and C represents the height of the retaining wall needed or the total height of the steps between levels A—B and C. If B—C measures 3 feet, six 6-inch risers (a riser is the vertical face of a step) or nine 4-inch risers are needed. While the horizontal measurement of steps is shown on your landscape plan, drawing the vertical detail (cross-section) on another piece of paper or, better still, at the edge of the plan and at a larger scale will ensure greater accuracy.

After locating the house and establishing the boundaries on the graph paper, draw in entry walks, rock outcroppings, clothes and utility poles, incinerators, fireplaces, compost heaps, flowerbeds, all outbuildings—such as toolsheds or playhouses—steps, walls, fences, and all other measurable objects that are a part of your present landscape.

If you wish to establish contour lines on your plan—assuming the area is not too complex—you may use an ordinary level with a simple **A** frame which you can make from scrap lumber. The horizontal bar of the **A** must be perfectly level when you rest the feet on a level surface. Fasten the carpenter's level to the crossbar. Pro-

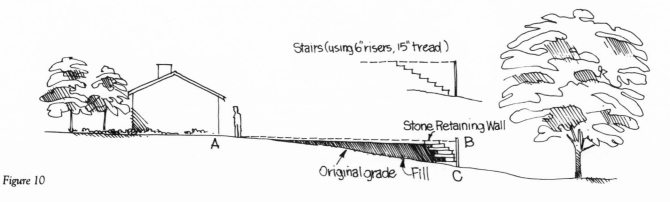

Stairs (using 6" risers, 15" tread)

Stone Retaining Wall

A

B

Original grade   Fill   C

Figure 10

ceeding counterclockwise across the slope, swing each foot of the **A** frame alternately and place it level with the stable foot, as shown in Figure 11. Plant a marker at each position as it is established; you will then be able to

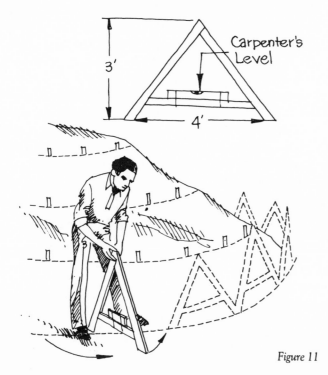

Figure 11

connect the positions in a line that is level, regardless of how irregular the slope may be. Often establishing such a line—being able to see it on the ground—helps to suggest the shape of a terrace, paved area, or other landscape structure or feature.

To locate and draw curving lines on your plan, such as major contours, edges of a driveway or walk, or the curb line if your lot happens to front on a curved street, put several short stakes along the edge of the curve, as shown in Figure 12. Label these A, B, C, D, and so on, using as many stakes as necessary to record the curve. The stakes need not be equal distances apart—their relationships to the base points (W, X, Y, Z) are what is important. Then, using the house corners again as base points (centers of circles), locate each of the stakes on the plan with the two-arc system used to locate the corners of the plot (Figure 8). After the several points are established on the plan, draw a freehand curve between them. You might waver slightly from the actual curve between points, but if the points have been correctly located, your paper curve should be very close to accurate. If a greater degree of accuracy is essential, increase the number of stakes along the curve. It is wise to double-check all measurements at all times, but especially in this case, and to record them on the edge of the paper—that is, A—W, 30 feet; A—X, 59 feet; B—W 33 feet; B—X, 54 feet; and so on. It may be necessary to use more than two corners of the house as base points, since you cannot measure through the house or other solid objects, but you only have to use one pair of base points (W and X, X and Y, or Y and Z) for each point to be located along the curve (A, B, C, etc.). A third base point could help you to check a point (A, B, C, etc.)

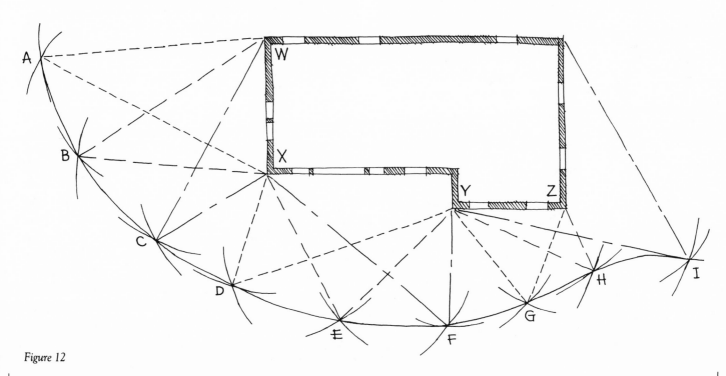

Figure 12

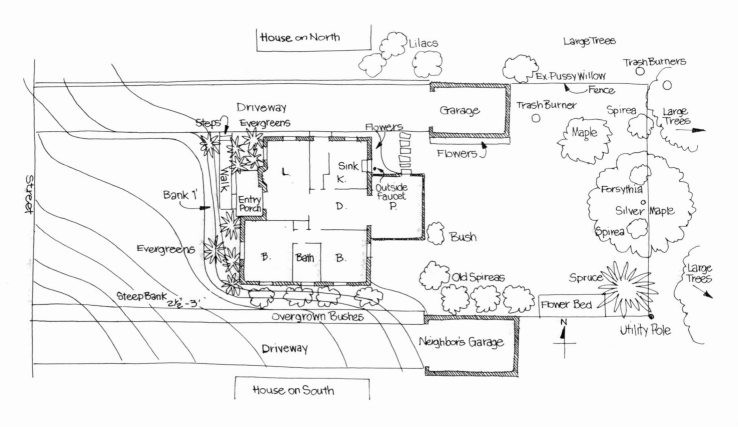

Figure 13 · Base plan: existing conditions.

House on North

Lilacs

Large Trees

Trash Burners

Ex. Pussy Willow

Fence

Garage

Trash Burner

Spirea

Large Trees

Driveway

Steps

Driveway Evergreens

Flowers

Maple

Flowers

Sink
K.

Outside
Faucet
P.

Forsythia

Silver Maple

Walk

L.

Bank 1'

Entry
Porch

D.

Spirea

Bush

Evergreens

B.

Bath

B.

Old Spireas

Spruce

Large Trees

Steep Bank 2½ - 3'

Overgrown Bushes

Flower Bed

Street

Driveway

Neighbor's Garage

N

Utility Pole

House on South

that becomes confused or difficult. Any other points may serve as base points (garage or barn corner, fence post, tree), as long as they are accurately located on your base plan. It is wise, also, to avoid acute angles such as YIZ; better to go on to another established reference point.

After the basic plan (Figure 13) of your landscape is completed on the graph paper, take it outdoors and check relationships of objects on the drawing to the existing situation. Have you put everything where it should be? If it all looks pretty good, you have passed the first test.

If you already have a survey of your property that shows boundary lines and position of your house, you will be spared some work. Be careful, however, if the document is a photocopy—be sure to check measurements and don't take for granted the scale shown because photocopies are often reduced from the original with the scale notation remaining intact. If your property is very steep, you may require the services of a surveyor or, at least, someone familiar with measuring and recording contours.

Before proceeding to the next step, mount a sheet of tracing paper over your base plan to protect it, especially when you are working outdoors. You can then make notes on this second layer of paper while reading the base plan through it. Later you can transfer important notes to the base plan in a different color than the one used for the base lines.

Landscape Analysis

While measuring, you may have given more detailed attention to your property than ever before; hardly noticed objects were perhaps suddenly important as it became necessary to locate them on the plan. Now, however, it is time to forget measurements and begin to analyze your landscape as thoroughly as possible and start thinking of its relationship to your family's needs. With red pencil in hand and eyes sharp, take your base plan and give your landscape an inside-out inspection.

First observe the view from all the windows looking out. Record on the base plan what you see—what is pleasing and what is not. Use symbols and arrows augmented with words to help you visualize and emphasize various factors. Especially with "picture" windows, you must pay attention to many factors—not only view, but also privacy and the degree of heat and glare from the sun. In the analyzed base plan (Figure 14), note that the summer afternoon sun is represented by a rough symbol

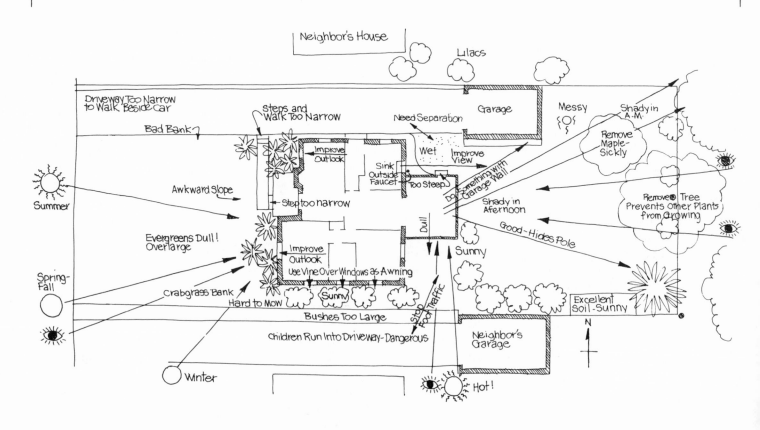

Figure 14 · Base plan: analysis of conditions and needs.

and an arrow showing the direction of heat penetration. Notice that the winter sun is also shown and that its direction is different but not objectionable, since the sun is much less intense than during the summer months and its warmth is welcome. Arrows attached to roughly drawn eyes indicate penetration of privacy in the living room and bedroom. An arrow pointing outward through the front living-room window is labeled "improve outlook."

"Step too narrow. Bank hard to mow. Evergreens too large, hanging over walk. Driveway too narrow for person to walk beside car." These are the things to observe and record on your base plan. Be as thorough as possible with all the details of the landscape floor, walls, ceiling—it will pay off later.

If, for example, as in Figure 14, much family activity takes place in the screened porch and in the backyard, your analysis should center on these locations; the views from the windows are of secondary importance. Privacy and interesting development are needed close to the porch. Notice that elements in the landscape surrounding the property are also recorded. (Your landscape is anything you can see from a given spot, whether or not you have legal claim to it.) In this case, the many large trees on the adjoining properties provided such a desira-

ble view that it was logical to remove the weedy maples and shrubs that did not provide enough shade or screening and prevented the growth of other plants.

If you compare the notations on the base plan with the final plan (Figure 15), you will find that a rope screen and wisteria vine were placed where "need separation" appeared in the analysis. Where "do something with garage wall" appeared, the planting beds were constructed and a color scheme created by painting the garage wall charcoal gray and using it as background. The planting bed and its contents take care of the "improve view" need at the kitchen window. The viburnum hedge and clusters of daffodils planted against the rear fence make the view even better.

The house in this example was built before World War II; later the back porch and double French doors opening off the dining room were added. The author lived in this house when his children were very young, and the direct access from the living and dining rooms to porch and garden not only made this small, ordinary house seem more spacious than it actually was, but also provided pleasant living in an attractive and easy-to-manage environment.

Developing a livable garden that would serve the needs of adults, four small children, and a dog and at the

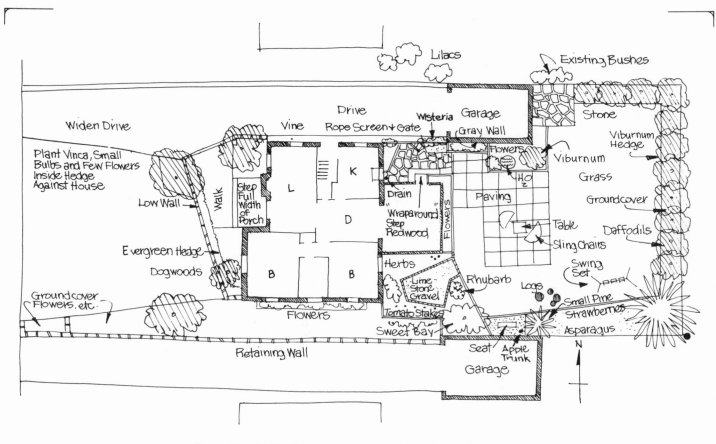

Figure 15 · Finished plan: correction of undesirable conditions and meeting of needs recorded in Figure 14.

same time would provide space to grow flowers, fruits, vegetables, and herbs was tricky. This garden furnished all these things by expanding the living space and creating a sense of enclosure.

To solve the drainage problems, ditches were dug and agricultural tile laid to carry off excess groundwater in a pattern that slopes to and converges along the lot's south boundary. All downspouts from the house were connected to this line, which drains downward to the street, empties into the gutter, and flows to the nearest storm drain.

Figure 16 shows a screen about 12 feet long. This was erected to connect the corners of the house and garage and to separate the driveway from the garden. The screen is divided into three sections: two end frames made of 2-by-4s, each measuring about 4 feet by 8 feet (the height is determined by the eave-line of the garage), laced with plastic clothesline at 4-inch intervals; and a center section, containing a gate, also made of 2-by-4s and laced with the same clothesline. A wisteria, planted beside the gate to grow up the post, filled in part of the screen and formed a canopy over the gate. The gate prevented children from running out into the driveway and from riding bicycles, tricycles, and other vehicles around the garden in an unrestrained manner.

Since the space between the driveway and the porch got a lot of traffic to and from the porch and garden and around the outdoor faucet under the kitchen window, the floor was paved with pieces of gray flagstone and paving bricks laid on sand over a layer of gravel (with a catch basin connecting to the drainage directly under the faucet). A planting pocket was left against the wall of the house, and the ground between the stone paving and the driveway was mulched with pebbles. This carried the stoniness of the floor under the rope screen, yet allowed water to reach the roots of the wisteria.

To make the elevated porch floor more accessible, two wooden steps were built over an existing concrete step, so narrow and steep that it was actually dangerous for small children. Crossbars from telephone poles (with the insulator prongs sawed off) were used to build a planting bed from the steps around to the east side of the porch, level with the tread of the bottom step. This bed brought flowering plants up to porch level for better enjoyment within. The steps allowed easy access in three directions—toward the backyard, the driveway, and the water faucet. The rear garden is a small step below the paving.

Other telephone-pole crossbars were used to build planting beds along the side of the garage. The long, narrow one is one bar, or 4 inches, higher than the level of the paving, and 8 inches above the level of the lawn. The larger bed is an additional bar higher, about 12 inches above the lawn. This variation in height added considerable interest to the garden. The well-drained beds, filled with topsoil and peat moss, became excellent locations for choice lilies, daylilies, and other plants. A large harrow disk (from a junkyard), with its center hole plugged and its interior treated with rust-inhibiting paint, became a birdbath. A tea viburnum, which produces especially abundant, brilliant orange fruits in the fall, was placed near the rear edge of the large planting bed, with a direct view from the kitchen window and the porch.

Bamboo shades provided protection from the sun in the morning and early afternoon on the south side of the porch, and the house itself shaded the porch as well as a large part of the garden in the late afternoon. While this garden, when completed, contained no large trees, those on surrounding properties contributed greatly to its appeal, providing a green background and helping to screen out neighboring houses, especially during the summer.

Tomatoes, pepper plants, and herbs were planted on the sunny side of the porch. A fence constructed between the corner of the house and the garage on the next lot protected children from the path of moving automobiles. This created additional enclosure as well as a rather delightful garden within a garden, which was defined by a central pattern of white limestone gravel bordered with old bricks and which contained a multi-trunked sweet bay and a large-leaved rhubarb. The welded wire of the fence (with squares too small for little shoes to gain toeholds) became an ideal support for various vines, including pumpkins for jack-o'-lanterns. The tomato plants were pruned to a single stem each and staked so there was room for six or eight, as well as half a dozen pepper plants, a couple of purple cabbages, an eggplant or two, a combination of dill and basil for summer salads, mint for iced tea, and a border of sweet alyssum and purple and yellow marigolds, whose bright flowers contrasted wonderfully with the ripening tomatoes.

A double row of asparagus along the south boundary of the garden provided a summertime hedge and good spring eating, the plumy foliage complementing the dark green leaves of the everbearing strawberry plants in front of it. Both extended from the old spruce in the rear to overlap the neighboring garage wall. This edible border-hedge terminated at a low-growing mugho pine

Figure 16

and another gravel patch. A 12-foot cut apple trunk, salvaged from an orchard at pruning time, with a pink flowering clematis vine scrambling throughout its limbs created an unorthodox "clematis tree" against the garage wall. Nearby, some tree-trunk slices served as seats, tables, and climbing blocks for children. Capped with snow in winter, these blocks, along with the mugho pine, seemed to be part of a poetic Japanese landscape.

The swing set and sandbox were placed in the overall scheme so that they had sufficient space and could be removed in the future and the grass restored without rearranging the entire garden.

The garden's back border was planted with a dull-leaf variety of viburnum, chosen intentionally to make the rear boundary appear farther from the house than it actually was. (The finer the texture and smaller and duller the leaves, the less conspicuous a plant becomes.) The viburnums were placed about 6 feet apart in a simple L-shaped line and were underplanted with daffodils and groundcovers.

All the materials used in this garden—old flagstone, paving blocks, telephone-pole crossbars, and limestone gravel—are commonplace. Few of the plants were extraordinary, and the perennials, bulbs, and annuals could be varied according to taste and interest. This was a very good garden for a young family, but it would work just as well for many other households.

Because you are working on a flat, two-dimensional plan, you may forget that there is a third dimension to space. This is particularly important to remember when dealing with sun control. Since sun comes primarily from above the garden, it is possible to diagram its penetration vertically as well as horizontally.

In Figure 15 the garden space on the east side of the house was shaded by the house itself in the afternoon. In Figure 17, the backyard is on the west side of the house. Unless protected by garden ceilings that can intercept the sun's rays, this yard would be exposed to the full heat of the sun in the afternoon and early evening, when this space is used most. The diagram shows how these barriers have been placed to provide the desired shade along with space for various activities.

The house (A) has its west window shaded from noontime and earliest afternoon sun by a leafy vine awning supported by a trellis over window (B) (Figure 18), and from midafternoon sun by tree (D). The paved outdoor living space (C), close to the house and easy to serve, is also shaded during the main part of the after-

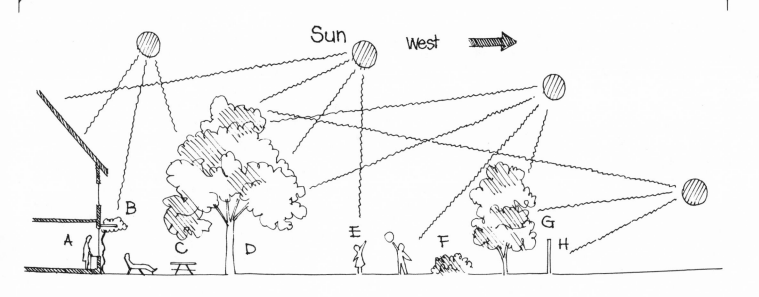

Sun

West ⟹

A

B

C

D

E

F

G

H

Figure 17 · Diagram for sun control: A. kitchen; B. vine "eyebrow" over window; C. lounging/dining space; D. large tree; E. open play space; F. flower bed; G. small flowering tree; H. tall fence.

noon by tree (D). The open lawn (E) is sunny. A flower border (F) provides a view of color from the window and shady lounging/dining space (C), yet is in full sunlight for most of the day (necessary for maximum growth and color). A small tree (G) and a solid or vine-covered wire fence (H) deflect the late-afternoon and setting sun, which would otherwise penetrate the outdoor living space by passing under the branches of tree (D). The larger tree also shades the west wall of the house for the entire afternoon, helping to keep the interior spaces cool. In Figure 19, seasonal change is diagramed to show winter sunlight penetrating the tree to the house. Such a diagram can also help you determine how to eliminate an unwanted view as in Figure 20, where the house is close to the street (and, in this case, where hot afternoon sun was particularly objectionable). Here again, compare drawing to analysis and final plan (Figures 14 and 15).

If you have trouble keeping the three dimensions of your landscape in mind as you work, build a simple model. Make a copy of the eighth-scale base plan and

Figure 18 · "Eyebrow" detail: a climbing plant (such as trumpet creeper or wisteria) is trained to grow up a vertical cable or pole and is supported above the window by a small trellislike structure that in time provides a living awning.

mount it on a sheet of flat corrugated cardboard or home-sote. Create the third dimension by cutting house walls, fences, and other vertical elements out of manila file folders that are stiff enough to remain standing and light enough for drawing windows, doors, and other details that can be cut out with a razor blade. Don't attempt to make a realistic or detailed model—you need only basic forms and shapes. Using your model should make it much easier to understand the relationship between spaces. When you begin to design your garden, you can

Figure 19

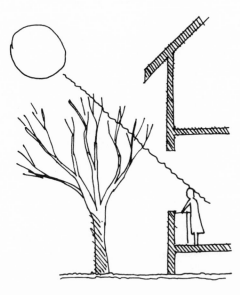

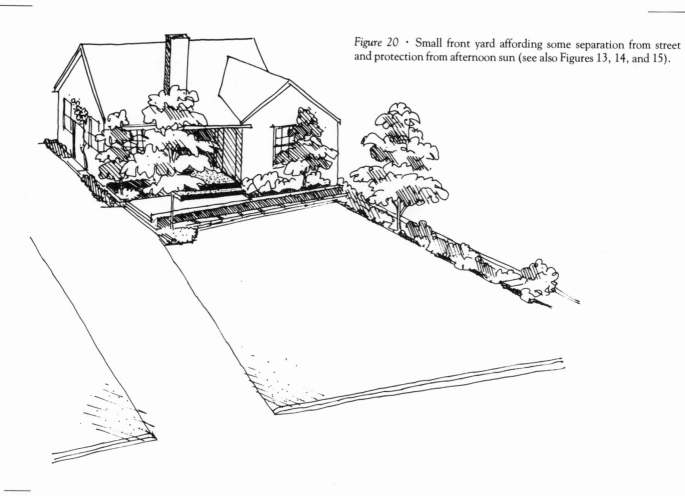

Figure 20 · Small front yard affording some separation from street and protection from afternoon sun (see also Figures 13, 14, and 15).

represent various objects with certain materials: red paper for paving, dark green paper for ground plantings, pale green for lawn. Sponge scraps can become masses of shrubs, and neat slices of sponge simulate sheared hedges. Dried weeds or very fine twigs can be used for trees. Use strips of balsa wood to build pergolas, screens, arbors, or anything else you want to represent. The model's success depends not on materials or details, but on the overall organization of the space. Remember to measure everything at the same scale—vertically and horizontally. Thus, if the plan is in eighth-scale, a 2-inch twig will represent a 16-foot tree.

A grid—a system of intersecting lines at right angles to each other forming a mesh of squares or rectangles (as in a crossword puzzle)—is a device often used by architects and other designers. Superimposed over an existing situation, the grid provides a useful framework with which to build a total scheme, provided it is suitably proportioned and properly oriented. It allows us to pick out blocks individually or in groups to create the garden floor. In some plans the grid is apparent. In others it seems to disappear completely, but it provides an underlying system that holds together what are often seemingly unrelated materials. Note the grid in the paving pattern in Figure 21; see how the outline for the

planting beds against the porch and garage are related to the grid and therefore to each other. Note, too, how "fingers" of lawn become integrated with the paving and the two elements become locked together.

I recall once studying what appeared to be a natural

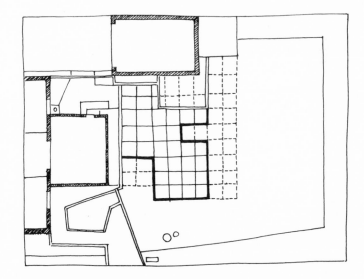

Figure 21 · Grid extended with dotted lines to show relationships between house and porch, garage, planting beds, lawn, etc., shown in Figure 15.

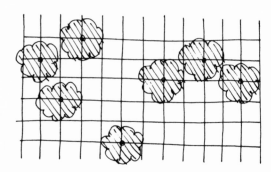

grove of trees (which I knew were only recently planted) and discovering that the very pleasant arrangement had been achieved with a grid. Although not apparent, each tree was related in space to every other one through the grid structure (Figure 22).

This basic system will appear again and again and in many variations in the examples illustrated in this book. Try to recognize it.

Establishing Goals

With the base plan and possibly a model finished and analyzed, it is time to make a list of objectives. Surely the analysis itself should have helped you realize some objectives. The whole family should be involved in the process and in assigning priorities if it is discovered that what everyone wants is not mutually attainable—for example, a swimming pool, a croquet lawn, and a tennis court, all in the same spot.

Don't plan small. Granted you may not be able to

Figure 22 · Trees in seemingly "natural" group; and same trees, their relative positions determined on an underlying but invisible grid.

accomplish everything on your list, at least not at the beginning, but that is where a plan returns dividends. It allows you to program the garden in a logical progression of steps. If, for example, your property is treeless and you are desperate for summer shade, planting a tree or several trees should be at or near the top of your list of things to do. And if you have planned correctly, they will eventually cover part of the outdoor patio or deck you plan to install in the future. In the meantime, the trees will be growing every year and developing that longed-for canopy of shade.

With a well-thought-out plan, time, energy, and money are expended in a manner that avoids waste and achieves desired results.

4 · At Home in the Backyard

We've examined space, our position in it, materials we can use to manipulate it, and techniques for measuring and analyzing it. By now we should have a substantial list of uses, comforts, and pleasures to incorporate in our gardens.

If we are going to make "order out of chaos," we need a system. The basic grid will serve as that system. It can be composed of squares, rectangles, or hexagons, and may be twisted or tilted, sometimes more than once in a single plan. If your instinctive reaction is to rebel against any structured system, remember that all art forms— architecture, music, painting—are based on a structural system, and are judged by the skill with which the system is manipulated.

Note how, in Figure 23, the underlying grid provides the system upon which hedges, fence, paving, and trees are placed. We are given a basic house plan in which the kitchen, dining room, and living room open to the east

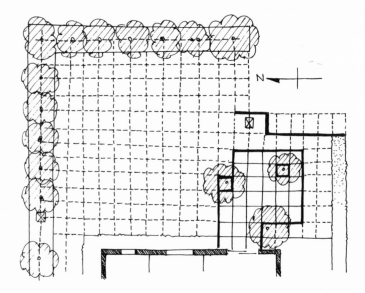

Figure 23 · Basic backyard, with grid system for locating various elements.

and overlook the backyard. The portion of the garden floor immediately adjacent to the living room is paved. The grid helps determine the shape of the paved area, which acts as an extension of the house and establishes a relationship between the house and the trees. The tree canopy provides shade, shelter, and a garden ceiling over the most-used portion of the outdoor living space.

This basic scheme can be used to develop a workable design in all of the following situations:

- a suburban or development lot
- a narrow city lot with a very shallow backyard
- a narrow city lot with a deep backyard
- a large suburban or country lot that is next to or part of a farm
- a large suburban or country lot that is next to or part of a nursery, tree farm, or orchard
- a woodland site

In the city or small suburban lots, the most efficient organization of space depends on recognizing the basic geometry created by property lines. In larger lots, boundary lines are not as apparent and have less influence on design than do important view lines or vistas. In these latter cases, the grid can be "tilted" to force attention in the desired direction. With small or oddly shaped properties, it may also be possible to relate the house to the overall property by manipulating the grid so that it reflects one or more obvious boundary lines.

Suburban or Development Backyard
· Figure 24 ·

In this small suburban lot, approximately 90 feet wide, we are confined by the property lines 18 to 20 feet from either side of the house. (We assume that the houses on each side are equally close to their property lines.) On the boundary nearest the paving, we have established privacy with a dense evergreen hedge and 6-foot-high sections of fencing. The paving, hedge, and fence are tied together with groundcover planting, which can be carpetlike and evergreen or a combination of various flowering plants, ferns, and dwarf shrubs.

On the boundary opposite the evergreen hedge are four sections of fencing and a line of deciduous shrubs or small trees that form a natural hedgerow. The fencing near the paving and the panels on the opposite side of the lot provide a connection with the evergreen and shrub hedges while providing more privacy than would the shrub hedge by itself. It is also an excellent backdrop for a piece of sculpture, a special rock formation, a sundial, or a birdbath or feeder.

Paving and lawn are at the same level, so access is easy and unobstructed. The deciduous tree or shrub hedge continues in the form of an **L** at the rear of the plot, limiting visual penetration from that direction. The rear boundary of the property can be immediately behind the shrub hedge or much farther back—it doesn't really matter. The open, unplanted lawn behind the fence and tree hedge can be used for a play area, a vegetable garden, or a pool. L-shaped garden walls are very useful (note that the hedge-fence combination near the paving is also basically an **L** shape); overlapping **L**'s provide privacy without absolute enclosure (Figure 25).

If we were to build a simple model of this basic backyard, we would see that we have created two related yet distinct roomlike spaces outdoors. The smaller and more intimate space is just a step away from the living room. It is defined by hedge, fence, house wall, paving, and tree canopy. From here we move to the more open, less restricted lawn. The gradual transition from rigidly controlled indoor living space through an intermediate, rather well-defined outdoor living space to the open lawn is well organized, encourages use, and provides comfort and pleasure. In the country it is logical to carry this progression further, through spaces less controlled and defined, until we reach natural, untouched landscape.

Figure 24

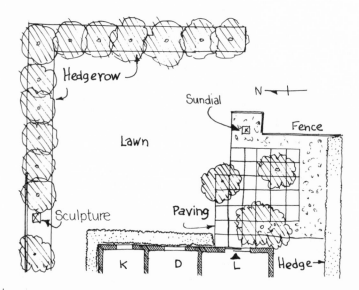

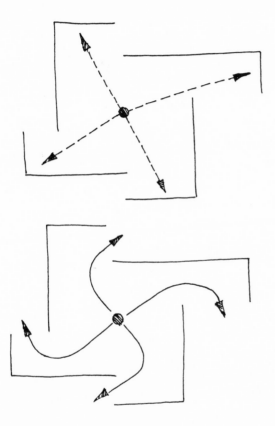

Figure 25

Shallow and Narrow City Backyard
· Figure 26 ·

We start with the same house, same three trees, and same basic paving grid. Note how the evergreen hedge has been extended to enclose two sides of the garden. The paving is flush against the hedge, leaving no room for groundcover or flowering plants. To gain some illusion of spaciousness, a low bed of flowering plants (roses are a good choice, since they grow well in the city) has been established against two fence panels on the north boundary. This attracts our attention away from the closer hedge wall. Another bed of plants and groundcover is found against the house. Both beds and the patch of groundcover under the largest tree are defined by low hedges.

Here we have created a garden that is distinctly roomlike, yet not as confining as a room indoors. The space is subdivided so that the paved portion is more enclosed than the lawn. In the suburban backyard, because of the shape variations within the garden, our lines of sight were encouraged in several directions. In this tiny city garden, however, once we step out the door our eyes are directed to the left, to promote the longest possible vista and reap every ounce of benefit within the existing limitations. The clean and uncluttered shape of the lawn gives it the illusion of spaciousness although it actually covers only a small area. This garden and the inside room together create a comfortable, intimate, and convenient space in which to live and entertain.

Deep and Narrow City Backyard
• *Figures 27 and 28* •

If a lot is exceptionally deep and narrow, its side boundaries are accentuated and we may feel that we're confined in a narrow passageway. This can be overcome by compartmentalizing the garden. For this lot, we have used hedge, fence, trees, lawn, and paving to define a strong roomlike space near the house, in a manner similar to the preceding examples. The long portion of the property is obscured and attention is held within the space closest to the house.

The rather traditional parallel planting beds in Figure 27 can be planted with roses, herbs, flowering annuals, or perennials. The placement of the four trees in a square

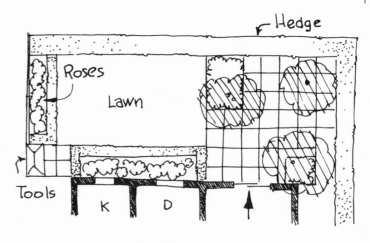

Figure 26

close to the house in Figure 28 establishes a stable force which counteracts the pull of the deep lot. This occurs because, like circles, squares have an obvious core or center. Imagine a flat and grassy prairie containing a square of four trees. It would be difficult not to move toward the square, because of the promise of shelter and being able to define our position within the vast, seemingly unstructured space of the prairie.

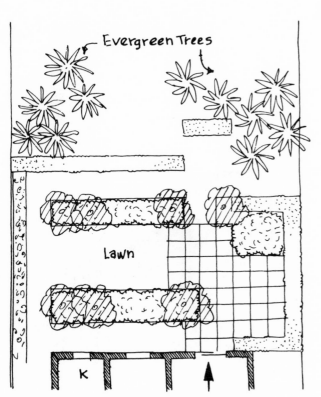

Evergreen Trees

Lawn

k

Figure 27

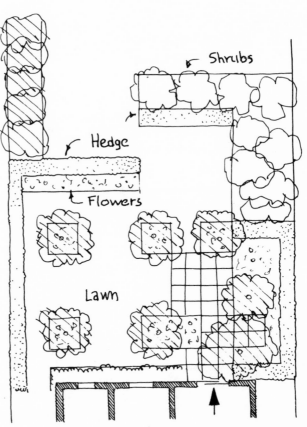

Shrubs

Hedge

Flowers

Lawn

Figure 28

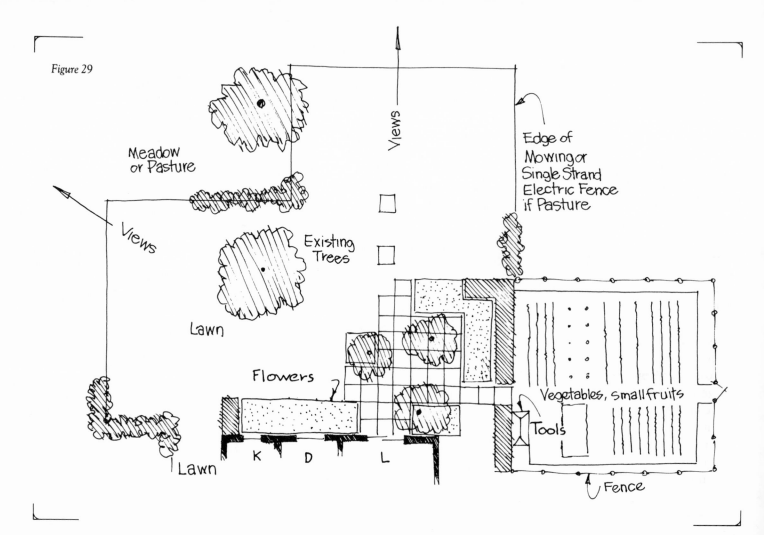

Figure 29

Views

Meadow or Pasture

Edge of Mowing or Single Strand Electric Fence if Pasture

Views

Existing Trees

Lawn

Flowers

Vegetables, small fruits

Tools

K   D   L

Lawn

Fence

Suburban *or Country Backyard* *Next to or Part of a Farm*
· *Figures 29 and 30* ·

Visual enclosure is less necessary in the country than in the city or suburbs. Close or distant views of cattle pastures, woodland, or interesting buildings become part of the garden scheme. In these lots we have extended the grid to emphasize the "offscape," that part of the garden included as vista but not maintained as garden proper.

In Figure 29 the paving has been extended so that the two blocks seem to float in the open lawn, drawing our attention to the distant view and inviting us to stroll toward the meadow to examine the grasses and wildflowers, smell the newly mown hay, or admire a sleek Aberdeen Angus or Jersey heifer. The line where the regularly mowed lawn meets the rougher meadow grasses is definitive (and is also determined by the underlying grid). If the distant pasture contains grazing livestock, you might want to add a single strand of barely visible electric fence. A switch, concealed by a clump of daylilies, a rosebush, or some other low shrub mass, allows you to turn the fence on and off according to need. The place-ment of this low mass emphasizes the outward thrust of the main lawn and calls attention to the two views.

The large vegetable garden south of the paved area is an adjunct to many country houses. The hedge separat-

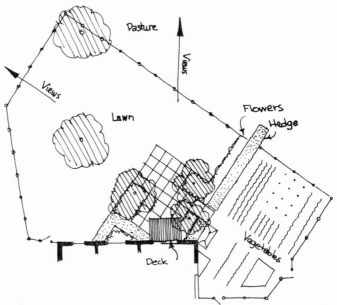

Figure 30

ing it from the outdoor living space need be only waist high, but should be evergreen to reduce the impact of the view from the living room during the winter. Note that the vegetable area is tightly fenced (those grazing cows!) and that a double gate is provided for tractor access so that (if this is a real farm) manure can be hauled in to till into the soil in the spring.

In Figure 30, tilting the grid draws more attention to the two large trees. The paving reflects the major direction of landscape interest. A small wooden deck, 2 or 3 inches above the level of the paving—and more a part of the house than of the surrounding landscape—establishes a connection between the house and paving. If the offscape is not of great interest, but openness is desired, a rail fence with roses, bittersweet, and other climbing plants will add to the outlook, provided they are not consumed by grazing livestock.

Large Suburban or Country Lot Next to or Part of a Nursery, Tree Farm, or Orchard
• Figures 31 and 32 •

These lots are very similar to those next to a farm landscape. Yet the structure of the orchard so accentuates the

larger grid that it is impossible to ignore. In both plans, a hedge arm reaching out from the house directs attention to the orchard and unites the two. The architectural shape of the sheared hedge dramatizes the irregularity of the trees in the orchard. Though only three or four feet high, the hedge acts as a definite wall, and therefore offers a sense of security. The blocks of pavement invite visitors to stroll toward the orchard, where flowering plants, ferns, and other types of groundcover grow alongside the path. Think how lovely the orchard would be, naturalized with thousands of daffodils.

Basic Woodland Backyard
• Figures 33, 34, and 35 •

Houses built within woodland are often awkwardly placed and unrelated to the surroundings. These plans show how the grid can be applied to the basic backyard on a woodland site. (The placement of trees is identical in both examples, although some have been removed in Figure 34.)

Because woodland is so confusing in terms of design (there are so many trees!), a sense of order is established by creating an open space that has a definite shape but

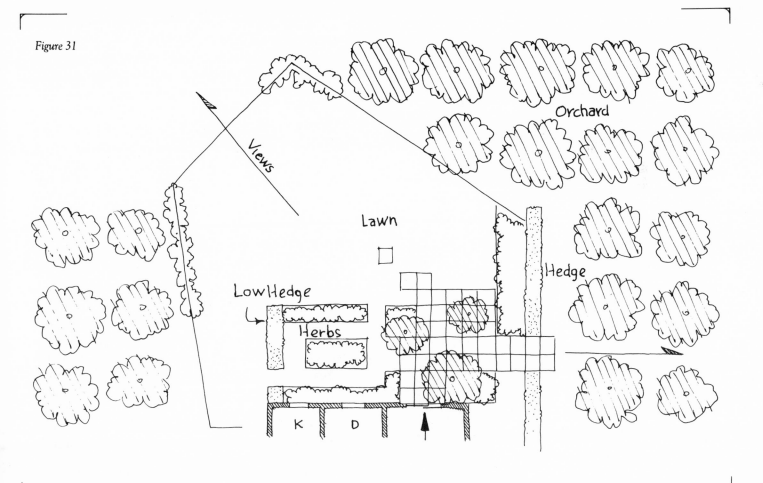

Figure 31

Orchard

Views

Lawn

Hedge

Low Hedge

Herbs

K   D

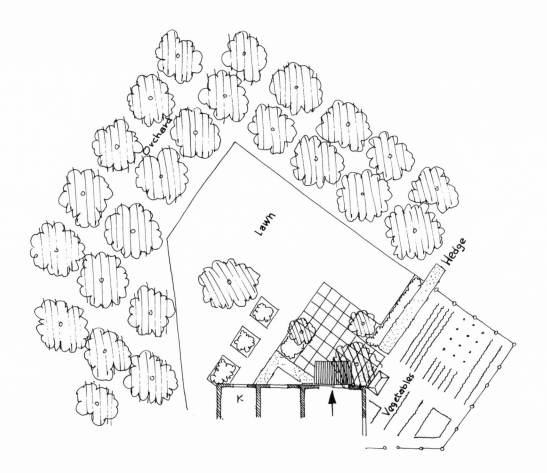

Orchard

Lawn

Hedge

Vegetables

K

Figure 32

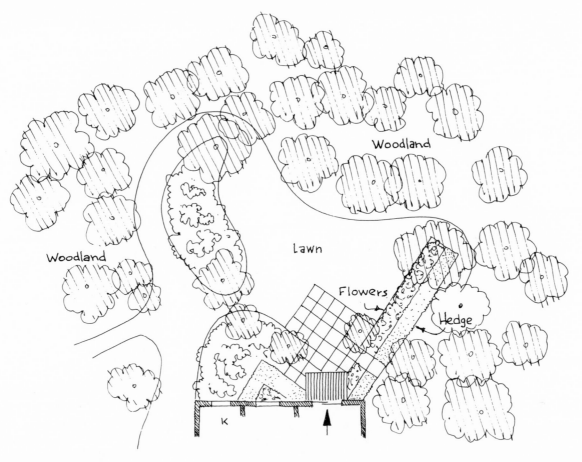

Woodland

Woodland

Lawn

Flowers

Hedge

K

Figure 33

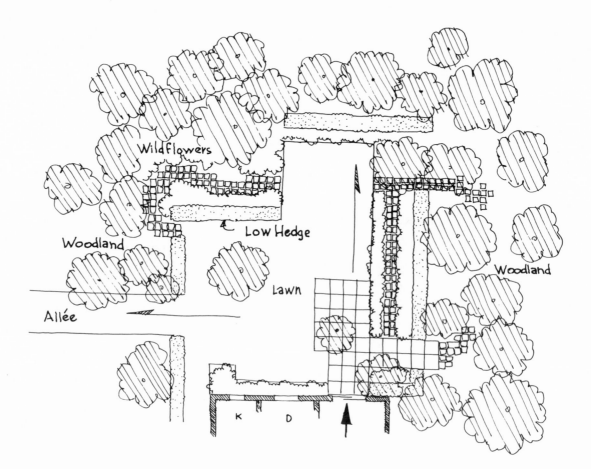

Wildflowers

Low Hedge

Woodland

Lawn

Allée

Woodland

K   D

Figure 34

reflects the natural position of the trees. Again, the grid provides the organizational system.

Natural mulch, mosses, ferns, and wildflowers grow freely at the edges of both the lawn and the pavement. The introduced woodland plantings can be limited to native plants or include a host of flowering spring bulbs, perennials, biennials, broadleaf evergreens, or deciduous shrubs. Woodland gardens are usually at their liveliest in spring; then they settle down to interesting green shapes, textures, and shadows for the summer. Unlike vegetable gardens or perennial borders, they do not need to be weeded or cultivated intensively. The richness of woodland gardens depends primarily on existing conditions, such as quality of soil, amount of exposure, and kinds of natural flora.

In Figure 33 the paving has been expanded and low clipped hedges have been installed to shape the transitional space between man-made house and natural woods. The edges of the lawn can be maintained in straight or curved lines. The straight-line approach is often better, since it creates corners and a more structured shape, projecting the architecture of the house onto the overwhelmingly natural landscape. The discipline of the straight line counteracts the unstructured abundance of trees.

The sections of low hedge in Figure 34 create a formal roomlike space from which irregularly placed paving stones form inviting entrances to informal woodland

Figure 35 · L-sections of tall fence break views and provide privacy (dotted sight lines), yet allow air circulation and free movement of people.

paths. An allée—a long, straight path bordered by carefully pruned trees and appropriate underplantings—is carved out of the woodland to add an exciting dimension reminiscent of ancient gardens (Figure 35).

There are many similarities between the woodland backyards and those described previously. Hedge's reach out into the woodland; the one in Figure 34 bends (on the other side of the deck) to enclose two sides of the paved area and establish the relationship between house, hedge, and pavement. Also in Figure 33, the wood deck again provides transition between the living room and pavement.

Row-House Backyards
· *Figure 36 A-D* ·

Many city row houses, especially older ones, have a basement half a story below ground level. In old brownstones, this was the original kitchen level, one floor below the dining and drawing rooms and half a story below ground level. As many of these houses were converted into apartments, the "basement" apartment was situated half a story below ground level and the "ground" floor apartment half a story above. The basic

grid can be manipulated to compensate for these awkward elevations.

Figure 36 shows four city row-house gardens developed on a grid. Garden A is almost entirely paved, with breaks in the grid for one large tree and smaller flowering trees or slender shrubs. A small amount of garden floor is devoted to groundcover, and the rear alley is easily accessible.

Garden B is similar except that a small area has been set aside for parking a car driven off the street via the rear alley.

Gardens C and D tackle the elevation problem. In garden C a deck half a story above ground level provides an overlook to a grove of three trees (underplanted with suitable groundcover), but does not impede access from the lower level to the backyard or alley. In garden D, the main portion of the outdoor living space is half a story below ground level. A retaining wall and flight of steps separates this space from the "stroll" garden, reminiscent of large formal gardens, at ground level. Plantings of shrubs and vines can be used to clothe the side walls and fences. A miniature vegetable garden with a useful cold frame is in the upper garden.

In all these examples, very dissimilar gardens were created and design problems were solved using the struc-

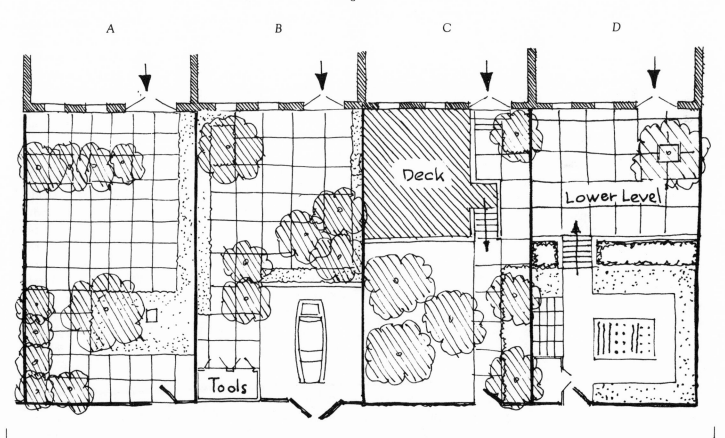

Figure 36

tural system supplied by the grid. Like most city gardens, these benefit greatly from—indeed almost depend on—the color and individuality of tubbed or potted seasonal plants.

Now that we have discussed how the basic backyard can be developed in various environments, we can consider how it can be modified to suit specific needs of:

- individuals or childless couples who want outdoor space for living and entertaining, one which requires a minimum of upkeep,

- a young family with growing children,

- a family with teenagers or young adults living at home,

- an amateur horticulturist interested in growing plants,

- a retired couple.

These examples are not mutually exclusive. Often they represent stages in the development of a particular family unit. Young children are not incompatible with guests or lots of roses—they can all be contained happily within the same garden.

Backyard for Singles or Childless Couples
· Figure 37 ·

Let us assume in this case that the occupants spend much time away from home, working or traveling, and have little time to take care of a garden. When they are home they would rather relax or entertain friends. Hence the simple, uncluttered lawn (mowed by a teenage neighbor or lawn service) and sparse planting. *Sparse* is not synonymous with *inadequate*, as long as the size and mass of what is used are compatible with the space. (This is, of course, our basic backyard from Figure 24.) The evergreen hedge of Japanese yew, for example, is high (6 to 7 feet) and dense, and needs shearing only once a year. A hedgerow of large shrubs or low-branched trees such as dogwood or doublefile viburnum also requires almost no maintenance. A thick mulch under the hedge prevents weed growth. As the hedge plants mature, the fallen foliage will serve the same purpose. Any carpetlike ground cover, such as ivy or vinca, can be planted against the house and around the trees.

The planting bed that connects the hedge, fence, and pavement may also contain flowering shrubs to provide seasonal interest. These can be grouped informally

Figure 37

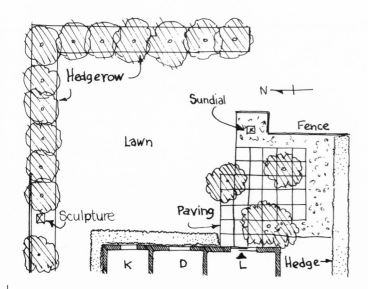

and combined with spring bulbs, perennials, and annuals (Figure 38A). Or the paving can be bordered with a boxwood hedge less than 18 inches high, with roses, mixed herbaceous plants, compact azaleas, or rhododendrons planted behind it (Figure 38B). A hedgelike row of azaleas with lilies and other tall perennials planted behind it can also be used at the edge of the paving. The high evergreen hedge provides an excellent background for the tall lilies, foxgloves, or other tall flowering stalks, including a formal row of standard fuchsias or lantanas (Figure 38C). The standards (plants trained in formal lollipop shapes) could be tubbed plants boarded for the winter in a greenhouse and set in place in the ground each spring.

In summer, potted flowering plants can be grouped on the paving with the garden furniture. Even if these plants are not maintained throughout the year, a quick trip to a nursery or garden center can rectify the situation in time for a party. Once a basic structure has been established in a garden, you can do almost anything within that framework—even develop a Japanese rock garden with dwarf evergreens in the area between the pavement and the hedge (the rear fence could be bamboo or some other material with an oriental flavor). A garden is primarily a place in which to enjoy oneself.

Figure 38

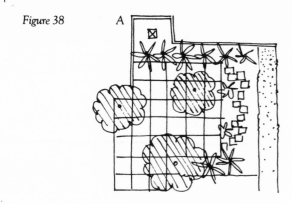

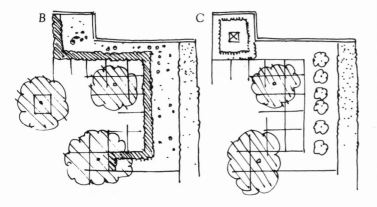

The overall structure should not restrict, but rather provide a framework within which to experiment freely.

In this basic backyard, we have assumed we were designing on flat land. Changes in elevation do complicate things, but given the same basic plan we can manipulate the grid to compensate for these changes. The grid becomes even more significant in terms of holding everything together. In Figures 39, 40, and 41, some blocks become deck, some stairway, and some retaining wall, in the same manner as the position of a hedge or fence is determined.

Lest you feel that the rigidity of the grid is too mechanical, remember that it need not be obvious. The choice and manipulation of materials will determine just how much and where the grid shows through. In the overall plan the lawn panel obscured the underlying grid that determined the position of the tree hedge. In Figure 42, the grid of the paving is emphasized by the framework made of 2-by-4s or 2-by-6s, which can be filled with concrete, precast paving blocks, bricks, cut stones, or irregularly shaped stone pieces over a sand

Figures 39–41 · (Facing page) Whether working uphill or down, the same grid system is applied, and all elements (stairs, walls, decks, etc.) are made to fit within it.

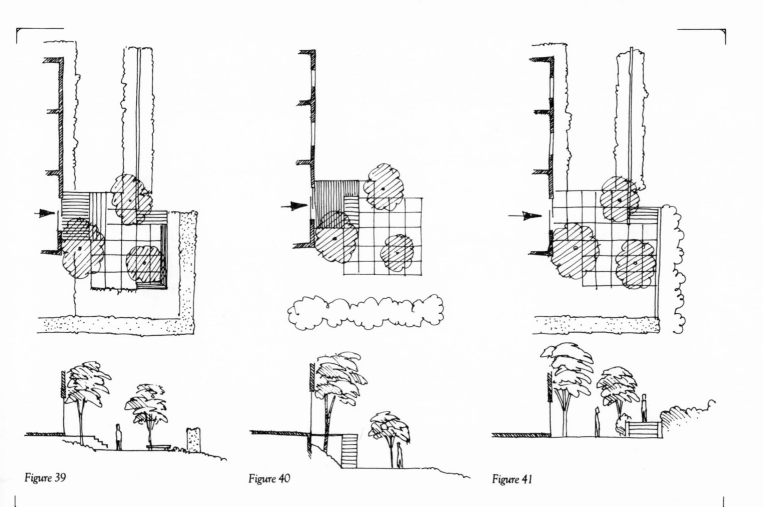

Figure 39

Figure 40

Figure 41

base. The blocks within the grid need not be identical; some can be brick and others concrete, for example.

There are many variations of this basic paving pattern (Figure 43). It can be reduced to two overlapping rectangles or composed of distinct, Mondrian-like directional dividers. But visible or not, it is the underlying grid that holds the garden together.

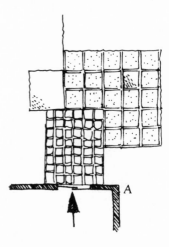

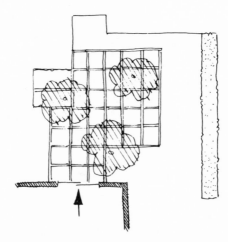

Figure 42 · Concrete poured into grid squares; lumber framing serves as form and adds interest. The same lumber framework, however, could be filled with gravel (as a temporary measure) or brick, cut stone, or paving blocks.

Figure 43 · Variations on basic grid for paved area (Figure 41): A. cut stones near house, concrete grid beyond; B. wood deck near house, gravel (excellent as a temporary surface) beyond; C. wood deck near house, paving brick (or precast blocks) set on sand beyond; D. grid broken into Mondrian-like pattern using paving brick with gravel or concrete; E. paving brick near house, random-cut bluestone beyond; F. paving bricks with large grass rectangle providing a green "rug."

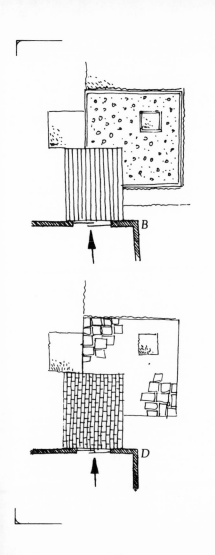

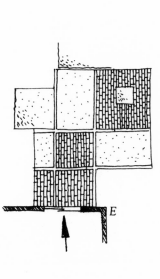

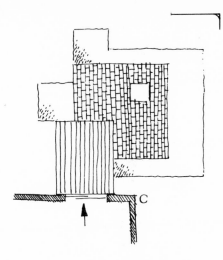

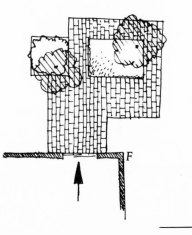

B

C

D

E

F

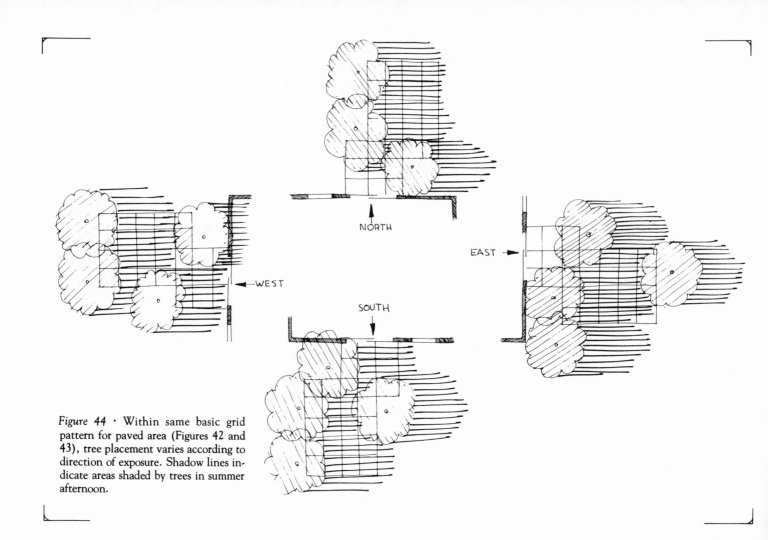

NORTH

WEST

EAST

SOUTH

Figure 44 · Within same basic grid pattern for paved area (Figures 42 and 43), tree placement varies according to direction of exposure. Shadow lines indicate areas shaded by trees in summer afternoon.

Remember that tree placement depends on compass direction. (Compass directions should be noted on the plan before you begin designing.) The basic scheme used for our demonstration plans shows a living-room window wall facing east. Tree placement will vary with other exposures, as shown in Figure 44, with resulting afternoon shadow patterns. The largest tree should be planted at the southwest corner of the paved area so that its longest shadow is cast in late afternoon, the hottest part of the day and the time when the paved area is likely to be used the most.

Backyard for a Young Family
· Figure 45 ·

Having small children is often used as an excuse for not developing a garden. But think of all the things about gardens that fascinate a child. Children are natural builders and enjoy being involved in the exciting and creative work of building and maintaining a garden. When my own four children were small, whenever we built a retaining wall, installed paving bricks, or dug a hole for a tree, not only did they participate, but so, it seemed, did all the children in the neighborhood.

The original backyard plan remains essentially un-changed except for the round plastic pool, swing set, and other juvenile paraphernalia that have been added to the scheme. A sandbox, with plank seats on two sides and a small awning to provide shade, has replaced the decorative planting bed by the fence. A square of sand serves as a beach for the pool, and another provides a base for the swing set, under which grass could never survive anyway. Though it may not appear as such, these sand floors are very much a part of the grid.

A household with young children usually has an adult at home much of the time. The small fenced-in vegetable plot in the plan can be maintained, with the children's help, as a diversion from household chores. Children often find vegetables suddenly palatable once they've had a hand in growing, harvesting, and preparing them. The center bed is reserved for annual vegetables such as tomatoes, lettuce, or carrots. The perennial asparagus bed against the side fence provides succulent spring shoots as well as an attractive summertime hedge. Since asparagus is a long-lived perennial, it will survive for years with little care if properly mulched and fertilized. Strawberries or salad crops can be planted around the inside border. The outside border of the fence is a good spot to plant annual flowers which can be gathered into bouquets for friends and brought indoors.

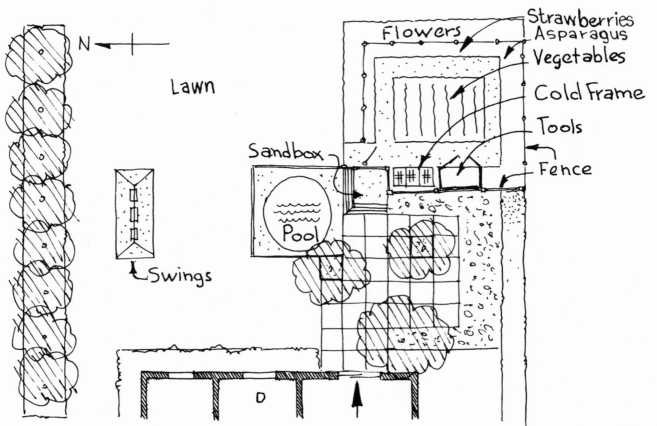

N

Lawn

Flowers

Strawberries
Asparagus
Vegetables
Cold Frame
Tools
Fence

Sandbox

Pool

Swings

D

Figure 45

The rest of the backyard remains as open play space. The rear boundary of the lot is purposely not indicated, because it is not particularly important. If the property abuts a community park or other open space, or is adjacent to farm fields or woodland, little or no rear barrier is needed. If, on the other hand, an unattractive building or other view needs to be screened out, the hedge and tree wall along the north boundary line can be extended across the rear of the property. If the view is particularly ugly, an unsheared evergreen tree wall can be used.

Backyard for Families with Teenagers and Young Adults

· *Figure 46* ·

Private swimming pools were once available only for the rich, but new materials and modern construction methods have made them widely affordable. Instead of rushing off to community pools or private clubs in hot weather, many families now stay home and invite friends to their pools. Because of this, the backyard has gained renewed emphasis as a center of social activity.

The basic grid has been altered to accommodate a pool. While it is not necessary to have a wide paved area all around the pool, there should be enough space for adequate seating. In this plan, that space adjoins the basic paved area (and occupies the spot where the sandbox once stood). Although a pool should be fully exposed to the sun for maximum warmth in the spring and fall, some protection is needed for comfortable seating in the summer. The pergola over the paving adjoining the pool provides some relief from summer sun. The diving board and deep end of the pool are positioned farthest from the seating area (and the house) so that people lounging by the pool are not splashed by divers, and children swimming in the shallow end can be supervised from the house. Large groups of guests gathered outside are less likely to be near the deep end of the pool, so there is less chance of mishap.

The vegetable plot is slightly altered, but the tool house has been moved and expanded to make room for pool supplies and equipment. The filter tank and pump are also housed here to protect them from inclement weather and reduce noise. (Noise can be further reduced by installing acoustical tiles on the inside walls of the pump house.)

The 6-foot fencing south and east of the paved area now extends along the side of the vegetable plot that

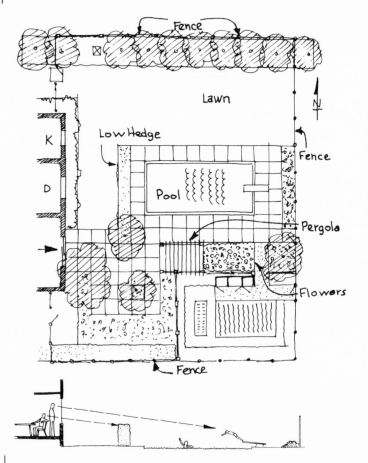

borders the swimming pool. This provides privacy and satisfies local codes pertaining to fences enclosing swimming pools. Using a high solid fence within the property does not contradict regulations restricting this kind of fence along boundary lines, although any fence bordering the pool along the property line must satisfy both restrictions. A 4-foot-high open chain-link fence stretches across the rear of the pool to provide the complete enclosure required by law. This fence can be placed almost anywhere, but should relate well to what is happening on the property and beyond. The fence along both sides of the property is obscured by hedge, and gates on either side of the house allow easy movement in and out of the enclosed area.

Although lawn clippings have a way of finding their way into pools, open unrestricted lawn beside some part of the pool is essential for teenage horseplay and as overflow space for large groups.

Remember that pools are not very attractive in the winter. Good visibility is mandatory for supervising chil-

Figure 46 · (Left) Backyard with swimming pool Cross-section of plan shows how long hedge screens pool from view of those seated, yet allows supervision (standing figure) when needed.

dren in the summer, but the need for some obscurity in the winter is also important. Careful placement of the pool in relationship to other landscape features is essential for achieving this balance. As always, view lines must be carefully analyzed. In Figure 46 the pool is not placed in direct line of sight from the living room; a low hedge and small tree screen the pool from sight but allow the colorful flower-filled patch beyond the small pergola to be seen when one is seated in the living room. The low hedge at the house end of the pool also restricts the view from the dining room, especially when diners are seated. Visibility from the kitchen window (above the sink) is excellent, providing an unobstructed view of the pool and the area around it.

We have again divided the backyard into two rather distinct spaces—the cool and shaded space near the living room, and the sunny and active space around the pool—yet they are well enough integrated to accommodate overlapping functions and smooth flow of people from one space to the other.

Figure 46 indicates a below-ground pool, but if the land sloped away from the house an above-ground pool incorporated into a wooden deck close to the house might be more functional. This would apply especially to split-level or high ranch houses that have decks at an

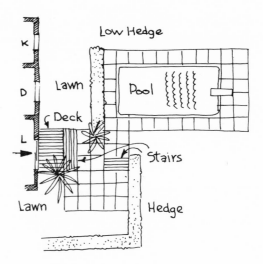

Figure 47

intermediate level between the ground and indoor living space. Figure 47 shows in plan and in cross-section how the grid can be adapted to a sloping property with an above-ground pool.

Backyard for the Serious Horticulturist
· *Figure 48* ·

This scheme is an expansion of the basic grid that allows for a great variety of plants. Since there will probably be more movement between the outdoor living space near the house and the vegetable garden than in other plans, the paving pattern provides direct access between these two spaces. Upon stepping outdoors, we can either turn left toward the hedge-enclosed flower border (which ends with a pair of trees and a piece of sculpture) or move across the pavement toward the long allée of fruit or flowering trees, which leads to a gazebo. Semidwarf apples, flowering crab apples, classic vertical pears, weeping Japanese cherries, dogwood, sweet bay, common lilacs (pruned to three or five trunks to create a treelike effect), or 8-foot-high posts supporting columns of climbing roses—each has a distinct character and creates a

very different allée. Only one material should be used, however, or else the unified impact of the allée is lost.

The ground between the individual plants in the allée can be covered with spring bulbs, ferns, wildflowers, or perennials. A simple carpet of vinca, spring crocus, and daffodils is lovely.

If you want an allée to appear even longer than it is, you can alter the perspective by bringing the two lines of trees closer to each other at the far end than at the near end. (Imagine looking down a railroad track. If the distant tracks were pulled closer together, they would create an illusion of greater distance. If the tracks were widened in the distance, the illusion would be reversed.) If the two rows of trees are 12 feet apart at the house end and converge so that the two trees closest to the gazebo are 10 or 11 feet apart, they would appear more distant than they actually are, although not conspicuously so. The path and groundcover beds must agree with the altered tree line, or the trick will be obvious. The grid should be adjusted in less conspicuous places such as the edges of the beds on the outside of the allée. Remember that as you walk back toward the house, the trip will appear shorter than it actually is.

Allées are often found in historic gardens, but they can be a part of small gardens too. In this plan an allée

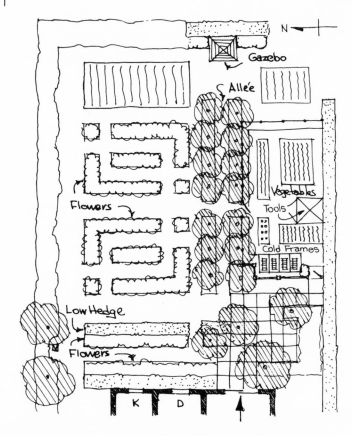

N

Gazebo

Allée

Vegetables

Tools

Flowers

Cold Frames

Low Hedge

Flowers

K   D

Figure 48

acts as a spine on which the remainder of the garden is hung, vegetables on one side and flower beds on the other.

The same grid that determines the organization of the overall garden allows us to cut flower beds into the lawn in a variety of ways. The straight, parallel beds in Figures 49A and 49B are typical and unexciting. Figure 49C shows the beds in the basic plan; the ones in Figures 49D and 49E are similar. All are somewhat symmetrical and centered on the cross-axis formed by the path that intersects the allée and leads to the vegetable garden. Figure 49F is not symmetrical. Paved pathways meander through and provide a close view of what might be plantings of herbs, roses, or other special plants. A rock garden, scree planting, Japanese stone garden, or pool for aquatic plants or fish could be organized within this structure to create a bas-relief on the garden floor. This composition can be integrated with the overall garden and still maintain its individuality. Another variation can be created from a simple rectangle (the total area occupied by all the beds) by making it a wildflower meadow. The relationship between this meadow and the rest of the garden remains definitive as long as the lawn along the boundaries of the meadow is maintained in clearly cut, straight lines. The meadow itself need be mowed only once a year, after the seeds have ripened and frost has occurred, to keep out unwanted woody plants. Daffodils and other non-native flowering annuals and perennials can also be naturalized in this mini-meadow.

This horticulturist's garden offers much room for experimenting and personal expression. The nursery and trial beds at the rear provide ample space for collecting, testing, and hybridizing. The gazebo is a comfortable place for making notes or conferring with other plant specialists (or friends) over glasses of appropriate liquid on a warm day. A gazebo can also be converted into a small enclosed garden house, office, or head house (anteroom) for a greenhouse, which should extend in a southerly direction to obtain proper east-west exposure.

The vegetable plot in this plan has been expanded with larger cold frames and a tool house. The nursery bed

behind this space can also be incorporated into the vegetable garden. The gravel or sand-covered paths within the garden separate the over-wintering crops and those that self-sow freely if the soil is undisturbed from the portion that must be plowed or turned over each spring. Cold frames can also be used for winter protection of lettuces and other greens. If the gazebo is part of a

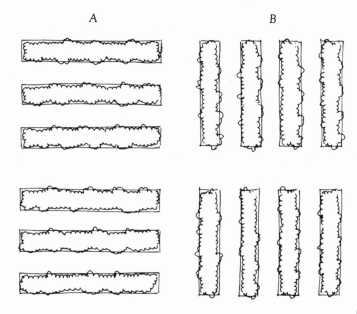

Figure 49 · Flower beds (for roses, perennials, annuals, etc.) cut into lawn in different patterns, using same total area. Variations C to E create interesting mazelike spaces. F shows a paved grid from which squares can be eliminated to provide planting areas for herbs, roses, perennials, or even salad vegetables. (Imagine it filled with tulips in May, annuals in summer, and chrysanthemums in fall.) All are segments of the same grid.

greenhouse, it should be directly accessible to this portion of the garden.

Vegetable plots and other heavily cultivated portions of the garden are not at their best during the winter. Clean or neatly mulched flower beds with neatly defined edges improve the overall appearance of this part of the garden. The basic organization is most evident in the winter when foliage is off the trees and herbaceous plants are dormant.

Backyard for Retired Couples

Retired people usually have a lot of free time. Since outdoor exercising is generally healthful, gardening is an

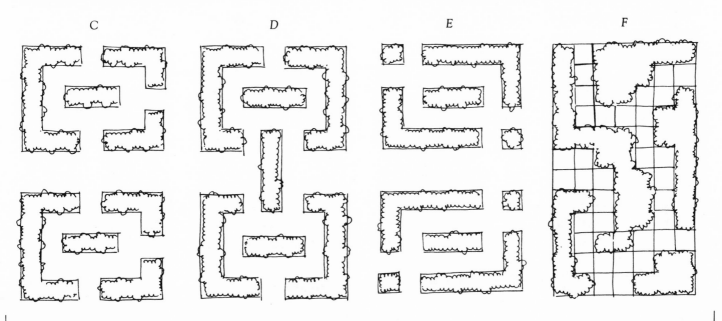

C D E F

excellent way to spend some of that time. (If you're retired and thinking of spending extensive time traveling, do it in the fall and winter—enjoying other people's gardens in warm climates—so you'll be home to cultivate your own backyard in the spring and summer.)

If your backyard scheme has gotten so complicated that it requires more physical energy to maintain it than you feel you have to exert, now is the time to simplify by removing flower beds, planting evergreen groundcovers under trees, and limiting small flowering plants to things in pots and tubs on the terrace in the manner of the first backyard plan (Figure 37).

Retirement provides an opportunity to give your pool—which probably hasn't been used as much since the kids grew up and moved out—a second life. Your grandchildren will probably enjoy the pool as much as your own children did. Although a functioning pool requires constant maintenance, it is not difficult work. (A professional service can be brought in once a year to do the major repairs and cleaning.)

The serious horticulturist with a heavily cultivated garden may be forced to make certain compromises as he or she grows older, but if the basic structure of the garden has not been violated by adding dabs and frills (something horticulturists are prone to do), this should not be too great a sacrifice. The great variety of plants or those types of collections that are very difficult to take care of should be relinquished first. (Individual prized plants or collections can be sold or donated to responsible parks and other institutions for public enjoyment.) The beds in the garden can be gradually converted to mixed plantings of vinca, pachysandra, or other plants that require almost no attention once they mature. Other beds and nursery plots can be converted to lawn or an easy-to-maintain meadow filled with daises, sweet rocket, black-eyed Susans, purple asters, goldenrod, or a variety of other wildflowers that help satisfy a plant lover's need. Wildflower seeds can be bought or gathered naturally by noting patches of asters, goldenrod, or other plants when they bloom, then returning to gather seeds as they ripen. Scatter this fresh seed directly on the new meadow and allow the rain, snow, and seasonal temperature changes to do your gardening for you. For an exotic touch, try introducing flowers not native to the locale.

5 · Reclaiming the Front Yard

If backyards are one of our most poorly used resources, front yards are even more of a wasteland. Our notion that front yards should be open and all-revealing may be a holdover from the pioneering days and a reflection of the desire to own land. Home ownership has been and in many ways continues to be the great American dream, and pride encourages us to show off so that everyone can see our houses.

Americans are by nature friendly people who tend to feel undemocratic when they close other people out. I remember a student from England who was astonished by the openness of our suburban landscapes and within our homes, where doors between rooms are usually left open. Generations of crowded Europeans have tended to compartmentalize their indoor spaces, keeping doors closed whenever possible. It is only in the last quarter century that we have begun to feel population pressures in America, yet this has created a marked decrease in our

willingness to be as open in mind and spirit as we have been in the past.

Any real-estate agent will tell you that, by and large, a house is bought on the basis of its facade, how it looks from the street. Most buyers want an impressive facade and will sacrifice interior space, an interesting landscape, or pleasant exposures and views to put up a good front. This kind of thinking encourages the tacked-on kind of architecture that is rampant in this country.

Showy foundation plantings are another sore spot. These can be traced to the development of the hot-air furnace. Since hot air moves up and cold down, the vertical systems that support hot-air furnaces must be housed in deep basements. American ingenuity being what it is, instead of digging a deeper hole for the cellar, the foundation was built several feet above ground level with the house on top of it. (Many Victorian and early twentieth-century houses are as much as half a story above ground level.) The portion of the foundation above the ground was covered up—with spireas, junipers, or mock oranges. This superficial decorative approach is still with us today.

Another noticeable but less entrenched remnant of times past is a garage placed far from the house. Barns were built far from houses because no one wanted a horse, with its attendant flies and odors, near the house. Naturally, it made sense to keep the buggy in the barn near the horse. When horses and buggies became obsolete, cars were stored in the space formerly occupied by the buggies. But it is no longer logical to build a garage where a barn would have stood a century ago. Besides being inconvenient, much premium land is wasted on an unnecessarily long driveway. Yet the influence of tradition was strong, and acceptance of houses with "attached garages" came about slowly. Actually, the garage should be as far forward as possible to give up as little land as necessary to the automobile.

We must now examine the entire front-yard space, establishing view or experience lines to help make this outdoor reception space a friendly, welcoming place, and to restrict exposure to traffic, noises, and neighbors. We need to reclaim the front yard as our own instead of allowing it to remain essentially street space.

The front yards described in this book are really "dooryard gardens," a scheme that has been around since Elizabethan times. In Colonial America, dooryard gardens—fenced and gated to keep out chickens, livestock, and rambunctious children—provided convenient places for growing medicinal herbs and plants used for flavorings and scents. These gardens were located at the front or side of a house, often by the kitchen, and were tended by the female members of the household. Plants were often grown simply for their beauty, but it is amazing how resourceful our ancestors were in using many leaves, seeds, and flowers we now consider only ornamental. Although we are no longer dependent upon home-grown herbs or scents, dooryard gardens can be surprisingly useful.

Basic Front Yard

We will now establish a basic front yard, avoiding foundation plantings (Figure 50) because they are almost impossible to see from *inside* the house. Instead we will develop a front yard that can be seen from indoors and provides some separation from the street (Figure 51).

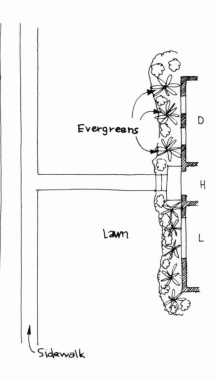

An evergreen hedge, no more than three or four feet high, defines an outdoor entry hall. A few small flowering trees are placed to give support to this roomlike space and provide an interesting vista from inside. Good choices would be dogwoods, flowering crab apples, and other trees that don't grow too large and dense and can be pruned to maintain a feeling of openness.

The space on the house side of the hedge can be filled with low groundcover and flowering plants, which will brighten the view from indoors and offer a pleasant and unexpected greeting to anyone approaching the front door. A simple evergreen groundcover, or a planting of low azaleas, daffodils, or summertime geraniums, can be placed directly against the house. Shrub masses at either end of the house break the view lines and keep attention within the yard while allowing free movement in either direction. This dooryard garden is an extremely logical transition space between the street and the house. The partially concealed space between the hedge and the house shelters a bench and adds to the anticipa-

Figure 50 · Typical foundation planting provides no view from indoors except of street. And the planting in this kind of two-dimensional "picture" concept can itself be viewed only from the street.

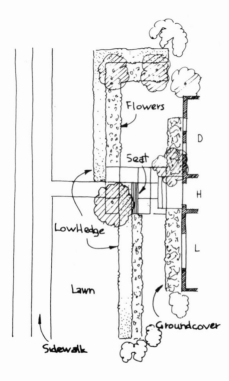

tion of a visit indoors. Once again, the entire scheme is held together by the basic grid system.

Figures 52 and 53 show how this entry garden could be adapted to a large country lot in a meadow or woodland. Parking space is provided for three cars, and the paving provides easy access to the front door.

A small city lot, usually limited to a front yard of only 20 or 25 feet, will often have a flight of steps leading from the sidewalk to the house. This change in elevation can be used to great advantage. In a city house close to the street, confinement is often desirable. Figure 54 shows a rigidly enclosed dooryard with an evergreen hedge, flowering trees, groundcover, and paving (possibly gravel edged with strips of treated 2-by-6-inch lumber)—no lawn. The edge screens the view of the immediate street, making the front yard appear larger.

Figure 55 alters the front yard so that the entry space can double as outdoor living space—often a necessity in the city—with enough privacy and appropriate views.

Figure 51 · *(Left)* Dooryard concept provides entry space—a sort of outdoor front hall—with an interesting view from inside the house, partly blocking out the street and its cars. It operates as a pleasant introduction to the house with its flowering trees, shade, and a sense of shelter within the hedge.

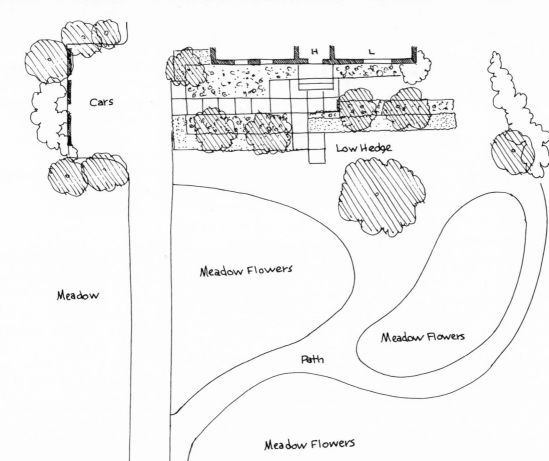

Cars

Meadow

H   L

Low Hedge

Meadow Flowers

Meadow Flowers

Path

Meadow Flowers

Mailbox

Road

Figure 52

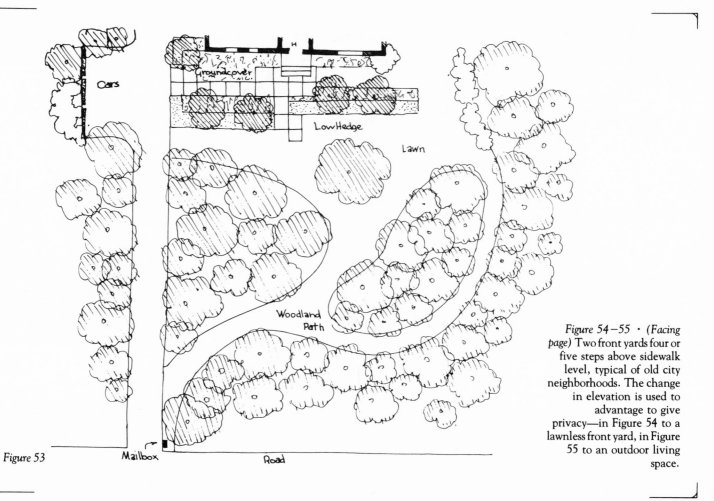

Cars

Groundcover

Low Hedge

Lawn

Woodland
Path

Figure 53

Mailbox

Road

Figure 54–55 · (Facing page) Two front yards four or five steps above sidewalk level, typical of old city neighborhoods. The change in elevation is used to advantage to give privacy—in Figure 54 to a lawnless front yard, in Figure 55 to an outdoor living space.

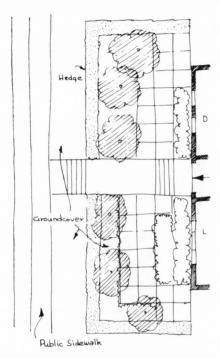

Figure 54

Hedge

Groundcover

D

L

Public Sidewalk

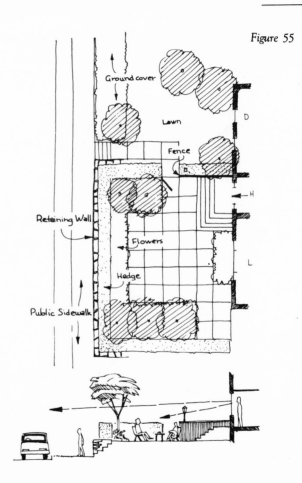

Figure 55

Ground cover

Lawn

Fence

D

H

Retaining Wall

Flowers

Hedge

L

Public Sidewalk

The wrap-around stairs provide easy access between the front door and the sitting space. Although both these plans offer an elevated front yard, they would also work at street level. In the second design, a higher fence or hedge could be used to gain privacy.

A 4-foot grid has been used in all of these plans, but this scale can vary from garden to garden. Often some existing condition will determine the size of the grid. If, for instance, a perfectly good 3½-foot-wide entrance walk is to be retained, a grid of 3½ feet per square would allow more obvious integration of the old walk into the new design.

Variations of a Dooryard Garden

The front yard is usually less influenced by family needs than is the backyard, but it is still worth examining how a front yard can be varied within the dooryard concept.

The plan in Figure 56 is in fact my own. When I designed and built the dooryard, I thought my approach was quite modern, but after I completed it I came to realize its traditional, medieval ancestry. The house faced west and the living room, overlooking the garden, was exposed to full afternoon sun. I wanted a flower-filled garden there, since the remainder of the property was wooded and shady, and this was the only place where roses and other plants requiring sun would thrive. I edged the flower beds with treated 4-by-4-inch lumber and paved the portion of the floor that did not get direct or heavy traffic with run-of-the-bank (mixed-sized particles) sandy gravel rolled to make it a stable walking surface. Low windowsills allowed a clear view of the garden from indoors, while the hedge blocked the street from anyone seated in the living room. During the summer the garden was filled with an abundance of flowering plants, but the basic geometry of the ground plan was dominant throughout the winter. The hedge, the large pine tree by the front door, the mountain laurel beneath it, and the evergreen ivy remained highly visible all winter. A large white pine across the driveway and several others belonging to neighbors also provided winter background.

After three or four years I decided to turn the center panel of the garden into lawn (Figure 57). I thought this would reduce maintenance by reducing the actual area of the flower beds, but that wasn't how it worked out. The lawn had to be mowed and raked and the edges kept neatly trimmed for the design of the garden to remain

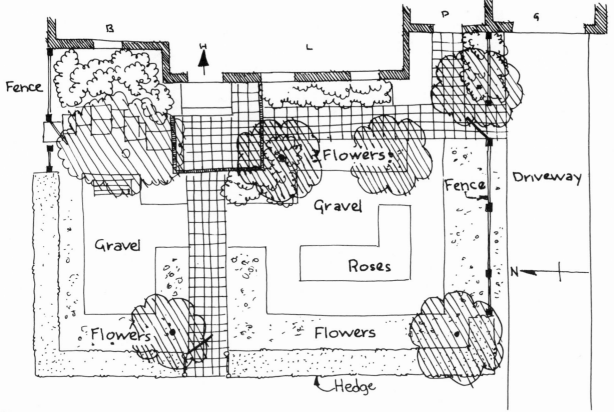

Figure 56

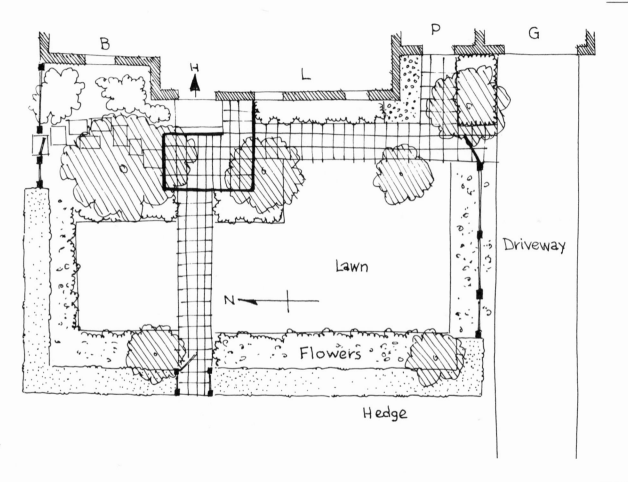

B

P G

H

L

Driveway

Lawn

N

Flowers

Hedge

Figure 57

intact, and for me this was much less enjoyable work than tending to roses, peonies, and delphinium.

The dogwood by the entrance to the breezeway creates a leafy awning and shade for the adjacent window (facing southwest), and protects the breezeway from intense late afternoon summer sun. A treelike lilac planted across the walk at the corner of the house provides cover for the front window, although another dogwood would probably have been more effective.

My dooryard garden was a great pleasure and I miss it now that I no longer live in that house. Passing through it as a matter of course every time I went into or out of the house added immeasurably to my enjoyment of the garden. I didn't need to make a special trip to see it. Part of the joy of having a garden is sharing it, and whenever we saw passersby peering over the entry gate we would invite them in for a closer look.

The following plans may be less of a horticulturist's delight than the preceding one, but may have more appeal for others. Figure 58 is a reduced flower-filled version of the basic plan, entirely enclosed by a fence of open rails, closely placed vertical boards, or some other material appropriate in scale and design to the house. Figure 59 shows an even smaller flower-filled garden enclosed by an evergreen hedge 3 to 3½ feet high. Both plans incorporate shade trees and groundcovers in the overall scheme.

Figure 60 is a still smaller plan; note relationship of hedge, sidewalk, and tree cluster. Figure 61 is a close variation of this plan, but the long walkway to the street has been eliminated and the driveway has become the primary passageway from the street to the house. The tree canopy at the front of the house is given special attention, and the trees are pruned carefully so that the view from the house is not blocked.

Figure 62 contains a grove of flowering trees, which provide a woodsy entry passage to the house and lead to a low, unsheared hedge near the front door. (In some of these examples the dooryard may appear to vanish completely, yet some enclosure is maintained, however indefinite in shape.)

Figure 63 shows how parking spaces for two additional automobiles can be provided so that no vehicle blocks any other. This is especially useful in neighborhoods where parking on the street is prohibited. The parking area is set off with hedges and the parked cars are further blocked from view by two small trees next to the window and a large shade tree near the street.

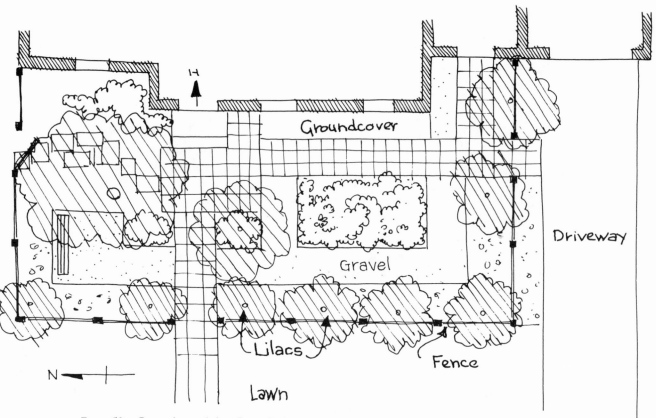

Groundcover

Driveway

Gravel

Lilacs

Fence

N

Lawn

Figure 58 · Basic plan with less flower-bed space, but thin open-rail fence and other materials.

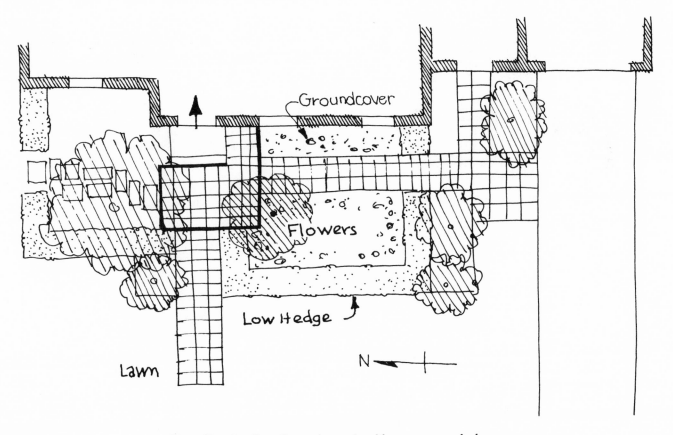

Groundcover

Flowers

Low Hedge

Lawn

N

Figure 59 · A still smaller garden enclosed by an evergreen hedge.

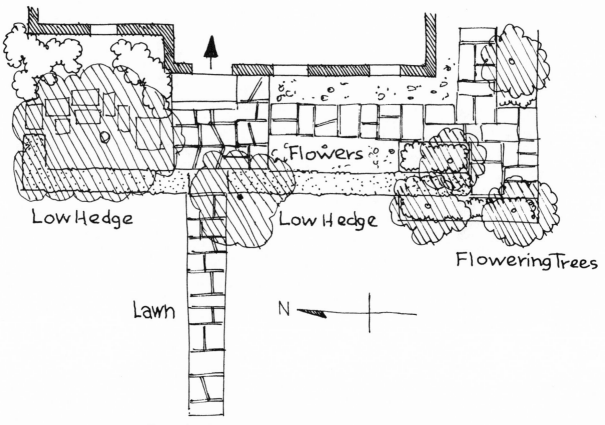

Low Hedge

Low Hedge

Flowers

Flowering Trees

Lawn

N

Figure 60 · Garden space further reduced, with tree cluster.

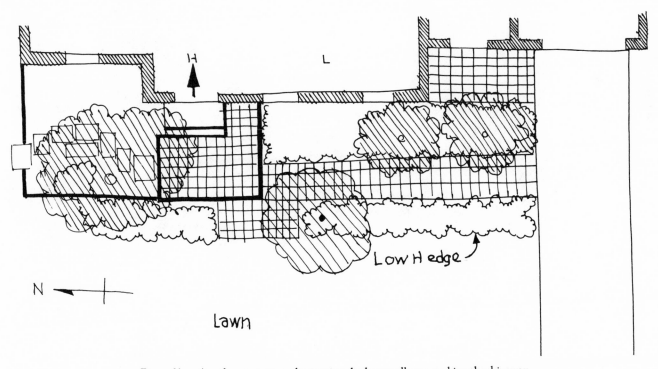

H

L

Low Hedge

N

Lawn

Figure 61 · Another variation, eliminating the long walkway, making the driveway the main passageway from street to house.

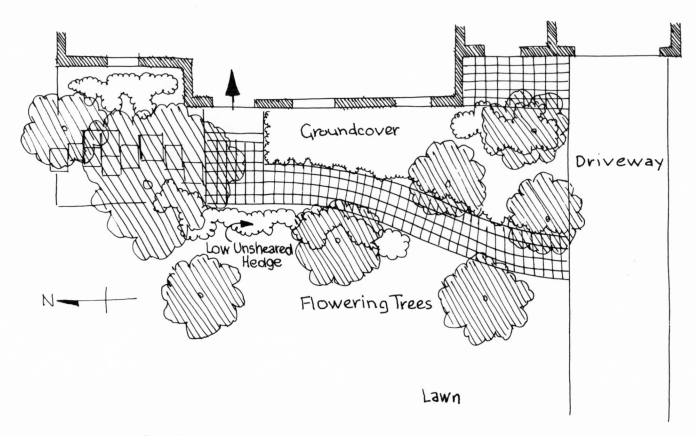

Groundcover

Driveway

Low Unsheared
Hedge

N

Flowering Trees

Lawn

Figure 62 · Still the same basic plan, with a grove of trees and a curving entry passage.

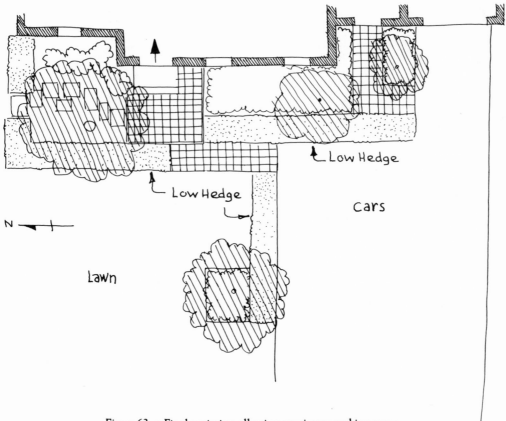

N

Low Hedge

Low Hedge

cars

Lawn

Figure 63 · Final variation allowing maximum parking space.

6 · *Lessons Applied: Variations on the Theme*

Some of the following solutions to basic landscape problems were developed by students in the landscaping classes that became the inspiration for the first *Budget Landscaping*. They all involve conceptualizing gardens as hollow sculpture and as containers for people. Most rely on the grid system, though this is not always obvious. Although these gardens are organized to meet specific requirements, the techniques used are timeless, trustworthy, and appliable to many landscapes.

Countryside Regained
· 100' × 150' · Figure 64 ·

After hundreds of houses, each resembling one of three models, were built on a tract of treeless farmland, the "green" that appeared in the name of the development was nowhere to be found. Instead of the usual foundation planting around the model house—of stone-and-clapboard Pennsylvania country style with an entry porch—a plan was developed to compensate for the lost country atmosphere and create some privacy, without relying on high fences and hedges along lot lines. Since the front view of each unlandscaped house provided full view of forty or fifty other unlandscaped houses, this was not an easy task.

The plan reveals how completely the inside-out, hollow-sculpture point of view controls the landscape. Views from every window are considered. Small trees (here, flowering crab apples) limit vision and provide an attractive vista from the living room, dining room, and kitchen. An interesting tree as a window canopy not only acts as an awning but provides a changing view as seasons change from spring flowers to cool green leaves, autumn color, and snow-laden branches. Two oaks at the

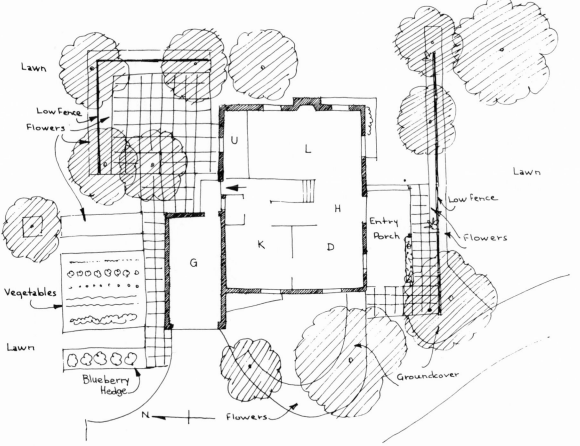

Lawn

Low Fence

Flowers

U

L

Vegetables

G

K

H

D

Entry Porch

Low fence

Flowers

Lawn

Lawn

Blueberry Hedge

Groundcover

N

Flowers

Figure 64

southwest corner of the house shelter the entryway and porch and protect the dining room and bedrooms on the second floor from late-afternoon summer sun. The large and small trees, paving, and groundcover all work well together, and with the hurdle fence they protect and enclose the front yard, so that the porch is not fully exposed to the street.

Unlike typical foundation plantings that run alongside the house, the groundcover in the plan follows the drive, linking the crab apple, oak tree, and entry walk and providing a view from the kitchen window to partly obscure the house next door. The shady lawn also gives psychological relief from afternoon summer sun.

Unfortunately, the designer of this house placed the utility room behind the living room, preventing direct access to the backyard—even though the placement of

Figure 65

SPRING

SUMMER

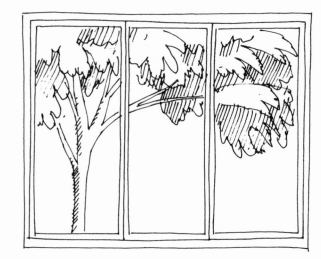

the house and garage, creating an already sheltered space, makes this the logical place for a small outdoor living space. Visualize this plan without the utility room and with sliding glass doors leading directly to the garden. A crab-apple grove (in the tradition of the medieval orchard) provides screen from neighboring properties; along with the flower bed, vegetable patch, and enclosing blueberry-bush hedge, it is a direct extension of the grid. Annuals, perennials, flowering bulbs, groundcover, and the flowering vines on the fence provide color. The remainder of the backyard is left as an open lawn play area, but could be used for additional plantings, a tennis court, or a swimming pool.

If a living space is functionally and comfortably organized, it should be able to stand on its own in both limited and vast landscapes. Thus, this plan can easily be

FALL

WINTER

adapted to an isolated house in a country meadow by creating a distinct line between mowed lawn and uncut or grazed meadow.

Split-Level Logic
• *Figure 66* •

Because the front of this split-level house faces north, the floor-to-ceiling living-room windows are never exposed to direct sunlight, yet they afford a full view of the street. The driveway, a few steps away from the front door and a level below it, doubles as the walkway between street and house. Whatever is done to make passage to the door a pleasant one must take place close to the driveway. The row of small flowering trees on the downhill side of the driveway (away from the front door) keeps the visitor's attention from sliding to the houses below. The crevices in the dry, 4-foot-high retaining wall contain small flowering plants, succulents, and small evergreens, most of which should be seen closely for full effect and are ideally located at eye level. The top of the wall is planted with sprawly evergreens that occasionally tumble over the edges.

Only a small portion of the front yard is given to access space. The remainder is part of the outdoor living space, either physically or as a visual extension through the living-room windows. The hedge, acting as an outdoor wall, provides necessary separation between the living room and the street, which is considerably lower on the driveway side than on the living-room side of the lot. A group of pines on the uphill side screens the living room from houses across the street and cars coming down the hill. The one pine near the junction of the street and the driveway further reduces exposure while providing continuity and balance.

Although the backyard is usually the most logical outdoor living space, occasionally a side yard is better suited. In this example, the rear yard slopes downhill westward, and to the south. Access from within the house is limited to a door half a story below the kitchen. In contrast, the dining room on the east side of the house opens directly onto a narrow porch easily accessible to the side yard, which is shaded by the house in the afternoon and early evening.

A side yard can be problematic because of its closeness to the street or a neighboring house, but the tight, enclosing hedge wall in this plan offers desired privacy and accentuates the pleasant view of the distant hills at the rear of the property.

The existing porch, twenty feet long and eight feet

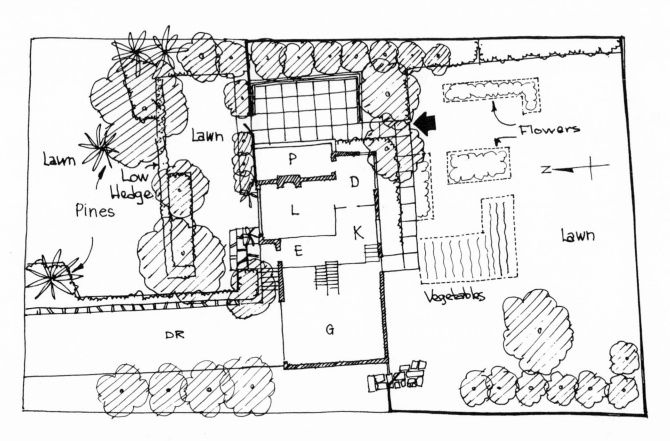

Lawn

Lawn

Lawn

Low Hedge

Pines

Flowers

P

D

L

K

E

G

Vegetables

DR

N

Figure 66 · Arrow on plan (in backyard) indicates view shown in Figure 67.

wide, allows space for little more than an uninviting row of chairs. Because the distance from the edge of the porch to the lot line is only 27 feet, the combination of porch and paved garden, partly covered by the porch roof and partly left open to the sky, provides for maximum and varied use (Figure 67).

Four-foot square blocks of concrete set in a wooden grid form an easy-to-construct and most practical paving. The area to be paved should first be excavated, leveled, and graveled. If drainage is particularly poor, agricultural tile should be installed below the gravel to carry away unwanted water. The grid of treated 2-by-4- or 2-by-6-inch planks is a permanent part of the floor, which allows for the concrete's expansion and contraction and prevents cracking. This grid system enables the do-it-yourself garden-builder to mix, pour, and finish one or two squares at a time. The first squares to be poured should be those that receive the heaviest traffic. The others can be temporarily filled with fine gravel until more time and money are available to complete the job. A few large nails should be hammered partway into the inside of each square just before the concrete is poured to guarantee that the wood and concrete lock together and the grid and blocks remain flush if any shifting occurs.

Although the porch is only about a foot above the pavement, a concrete step stretching the entire length between the two provides comfortable passage and unifies them. A wooden seat-wall mounted on ceramic chimney-tile supports defines the eastern edge of the paving. It also adds considerably to the seating capacity and entertaining value of the space while reducing the amount of movable furniture needed. And it keeps feet out of the groundcovers, bulbs, annuals, and perennials planted between the paving and the hedge.

A dense screen of doublefile viburnums planted 4 feet inside the lot line should grow to nearly 8 feet tall and 8 feet wide. The hedge continues beyond the fence at the front of the house and beyond the boundary of the paved concrete blocks at the rear, providing complete privacy and carrying the eye toward the distant hills. Two honey locusts planted at the rear of the paving provide morning and midday shade for the paved area and the dining room, while their trunks and overhanging limbs frame the hills.

At the front of the paving, a low, grated chain-link fence and multitrunked sweet bays (which bear extremely fragrant flowers intermittently all through the summer) offer protection from the street, while the evergreen hedge and Scots pines afford added privacy to the front yard and the living room.

Figure 67

The rear of the lot is entirely open except for an existing tree; the chain-link fence continues around the boundary to meet, with a gate, the garage corner, thus allowing safe and controlled play space for small chil-

dren. Beds for asparagus and other vegetables, roses, and cut flowers can be incorporated into the overall garden design and just as easily converted back to grass.

Although much of this area is not level, it is

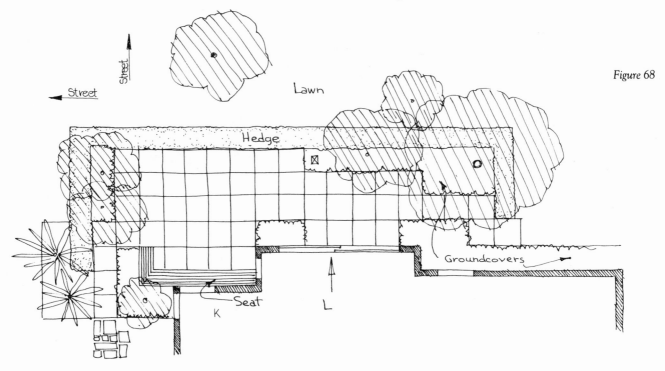

Figure 68

adequate play space for children or adults. Viburnum, lilacs, or other large shrubs or small trees can be used to block the house to the west.

On Two Fronts
· 200' × 200' · Figure 68 ·

All too frequently a large single-story house is set in the back of a corner lot, often because of set-back ordinances that apply in both directions and require that a house be a certain distance from the curb. This results in a two-sided front yard and a driveway and garage in the back.

This sweeping front lawn provides a pleasant vista of the house for passersby from the south and east, but no privacy. Evergreen foundation plantings ringing the house gave no separation from either street and left anyone within the house feeling totally exposed to passing traffic even though it was some distance away. To recapture some of the streetside space so that it could relate to indoor space, the existing foundation yews were pulled away from the house to create a 3-foot hedge outside the living room (Figure 69). Shade trees and small flowering

trees form a canopy over this space and shade the wall of windows. The flowering trees on the open lawn, beyond the hedge, effectively screen some of the houses across the street. The screening effect is less complete in the winter than in the summer, but since draperies are usually drawn by five or six o'clock in the winter, the view is less critical. And even leafless trees are more attractive

Figure 69

than bare lawn, especially if they contain birdhouses or feeders. Although in this case the garden outside the window wall was originally designed only as a visual extension of the living room, converting windows to doors, as shown, would provide direct and easy access outside. (If architects, builders, and would-be homeowners consulted garden designers before building, such convenience might be incorporated into basic house plans.)

The downward slope of the lawn is much steeper on the east (kitchen-breakfast room) front of the house than on the south front and faces a small orchard and an attractive old barn across the road. Here the hedge completely blocks vision of the road and passing cars from anyone seated at the breakfast table, but allows complete view of the orchard (Figure 70). The flowering crab apple within the yard provides a natural canopy and promotes the illusion that the distant apple orchard is part of the property.

With the new landscaping, the trees, hedge, and shadows on the lawn enhance the feeling that the house occupies its own well-defined space and is not a public showplace. The long, low hedges away from the house blend beautifully with the house's low, horizontal facades, and the vertical trees dramatize both, so while all landscaping was done from the inside-out viewpoint, the public view is also much improved.

This is again a grid-based landscape that works almost anywhere. The position of the trees could be changed in any particular situation to screen out unwanted views and provide necessary shade.

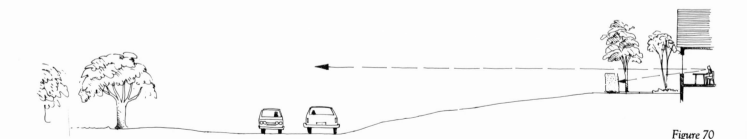

Figure 70

Outdoor Room
· *30' × 120'· Figure 71* ·

This spacious corner ranch house has very broad front and side lawns and a very small backyard, which is clearly visible from the second-floor windows of the house next door.

A gazebolike structure, only 16 by 18 feet, backed by an evergreen hedge, provides shelter and privacy. Instead of continuing the hedge along the entire property line, which would have been much too confining and monotonous, the eave line of the gazebo was extended with 2-by-6-inch planks to connect the 8-foot fence posts and create a support for flowering vines. The standard, prebuilt, woven-panel fence is only 3 feet high and is a much airier and more friendly structure than a tall fence. The fence's L-shaped turn near the street increases the feeling of enclosure and establishes a connection between the fence, the row of small flowering trees, and the low evergreen hedge that outlines the small flower garden just outside the living-room window. Although the fence is inside the property boundary and lines up with the *inside* of the evergreen hedge, the amount of space "lost" is a small price to pay for acceptance of such a structure by a neighbor. Besides, the climbing plants growing on the structure (grape, trumpet, creeper, or wisteria) will grow outward into the space.

Preservative stains are available in a wide range of colors and in opaque, transparent, or semitransparent finishes, so one is no longer limited to the harsh and artificial redwood color that comes on much prefabricated fencing. Buy unfinished wood and buy a color that fits the landscape. Usually the safest approach is to repeat or extend the color of the house—a very important element of the landscape. If this does not work, change the color of the house next time it needs to be painted.

This gazebo is hardly more than a sunshade. If zoning prohibits a full-fledged structure close to the lot line, a simple pipe frame supporting a colorful striped awning can be used. While it is nice to have something solid overhead to protect furniture from dew and rain, an arbor with climbing plants is another choice and still provides shade and protection from anyone peeping from the second-story windows of the house next door.

A storage wall—for trash cans, cooking equipment, and garden tools and furniture—at the left boundary of this space effectively screens the neighbor, and a miniature utility yard is enclosed with the same vine-covered

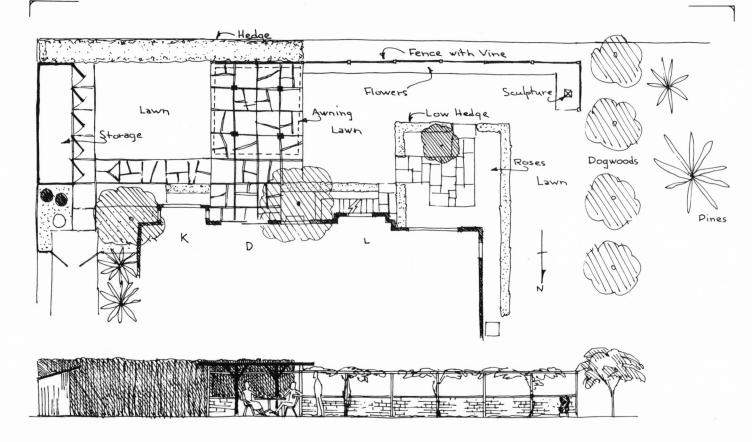

Figure 71

fence as that along the rear property line. A double gate in the fence opens directly onto the asphalt driveway. At the other end, a row of pines planted along the side street absorbs street noises and increases privacy. The view from the restricted roomlike end of the garden to the distant pines and dogwoods in front of them provides relief from the geometric quality of the space itself. Notice how the crisply defined lawn panels and evergreen hedge lock into the total scheme—the grid again.

Sunshade and Privacy
· 30′ × 100′· *Figure 72* ·

In this plan we began with a basically treeless lot where the kitchen, dining room, family room, and porch were exposed to the full brunt of afternoon sun, and there was no privacy. Since the lot is very shallow, enclosure and shade are provided close to the house in the form of an outdoor wall, consisting of a hedge about three feet high and a row of small flowering trees, to create an extension of the kitchen, family room, and porch spaces.

The Japanese tree lilacs provide a visual barrier and relief from early afternoon sun without creating a solid wall. They are inexpensive and fast-growing, reaching a height of about 30 feet, and produce large heads of creamy white flowers each June. The tree trunks develop interesting lines suggestive of oriental gardens. Other small trees or large shrubs—flowering crab apples or magnolias—with unusual trunks and moderate mass can be used to create the same effect. The evergreen hedge further defines the outdoor space and serves as a backdrop for the low-growing flowering plants and other groundcover.

Initially, the evergreen hedge is probably the most expensive investment in this landscape (spaced 2½ feet from each other, thirty yews were needed), but may turn out to be the most economical in the long run. Yews can be pruned back sharply and kept at the desired size, since dormant buds under old bark will produce new shoots and old plants will constantly renew themselves. (This is not so with junipers, arborvitae, pines, and most other evergreens in common use. After a certain amount of time their branches will remain forever bare and they must be replaced.)

In milder climates, boxwood, magnolia, evergreen privet, or several other evergreen plants can be turned into a suitable hedge. California privet is a good choice on a very limited budget because, although it needs con-

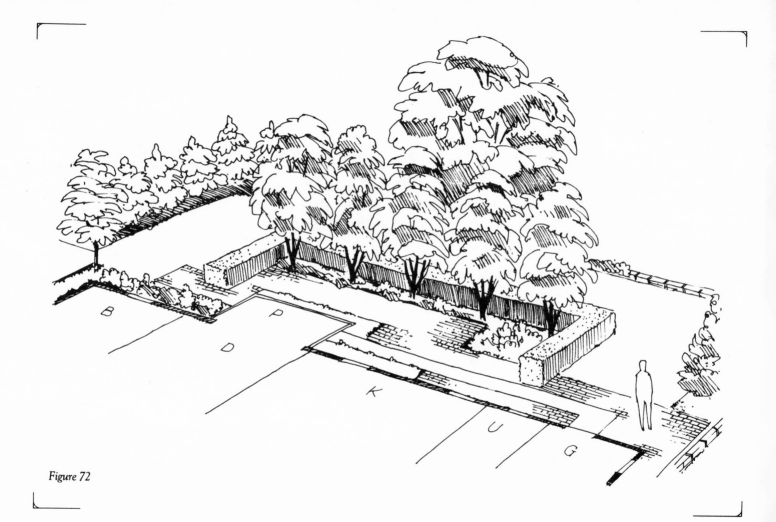

Figure 72

stant shearing, it makes a neat hedge that gives the desired effect within two years. Since it is extremely inexpensive, replacing it with a more desirable material after several years shouldn't be a hardship. Another alternative on a limited budget is to buy small-sized quality plants and wait for them to grow. Be aware, however, that it can take a seemingly endless period for a row of 12-inch yews to grow into a dense 36-inch hedge.

A 3-foot-wide, poured concrete walk was installed from the porch door to the service door when the house was built. But the grass on either side of the walk quickly became worn. To extend the paving, a brick border was laid on a bed of sand on either side of the existing walk. This brick paving also extends around the porch and creates a floor for the adjacent garden space. The utility area just outside the service door is also paved with brick, since this is the spot where lawn mowers are oiled, bicycles taken apart, and other similar activities carried out, none of them conducive to growing grass. These easy-to-maintain brick areas enlarge the walking, sitting, and working spaces while providing a good, sturdy surface for working in the flower beds.

In the flower beds, a profusion of spring bulbs such as daffodils and tulips, perennials, summer zinnias, and marigolds or petunias in sunny places will produce abundant colors that can be seen and enjoyed from indoors and out. As the surrounding trees grow larger and provide more shade, you can switch to more shade-tolerant evergreen groundcovers, ferns, and early spring bulbs.

Except for two Douglas fir screens and some vines planted at the base of the retaining wall on the property line, the rest of the backyard remains open and uncluttered. The firs are planted in beds cut out of the turf and mulched to reduce weeding and simplify mowing.

Maximum Function in Minimum Space
• 38' × 60' • *Figure 73* •

This small backyard, much restricted by a garage, contained a medium-sized apple tree at the back corner and a privet hedge. The hedge was filled in, retrained, and sheared at six feet; it was also extended to provide complete privacy on both sides. While in most cases a privet hedge is a nuisance because it requires such frequent shearing, here where the property is very small and requires little maintenance, it is not much of a bother and is an inexpensive and less confining border than an architectural fence.

The residents of the property were working people

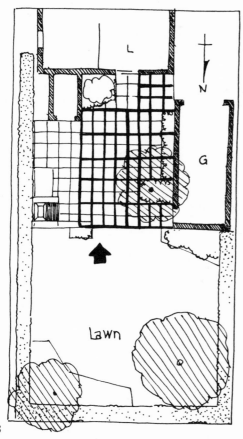

Figure 73

and wanted a place where in warm weather they could relax, cook, and eat outdoors after a day at the office. This required complete privacy, a durable floor, and protection from the sun (Figure 74).

The fireplace can be used for both cooking and heating, which makes the area more pleasant in the spring and fall. One side of the fireplace is constructed as a seat-high boundary wall, while the other side continues at counter level and provides workspace on top and storage for fuel and equipment below. Agricultural-tile drains were installed before the actual construction began to carry off storm water and provide a well-drained foundation for the paving. A pattern of 2-foot concrete squares was designed so that the squares could be cast indoors during the winter, two or three at a time. Portions of the garden floor are devoted to carpetlike evergreen groundcover and the rest to lawn, resulting in a floor pattern that is functional and interesting, though limited in area.

The garage protects the garden space on the west side of the lot from late-afternoon sun, and an egg-crate trellis provides additional shade. In the middle of the day the sun filters through between the boards, and only the narrow edges of the vertical boards cast shadows on the paving; but as the sun moves westward the boards of the

Figure 74

trellis cast ever wider shadows. By four or five o'clock in the afternoon, the terrace is almost entirely shaded. The addition of vines provides shade earlier in the day. Air circulates through the vines to keep the enclosed space cool and dry. A large opening is left in the trellis to allow a birch tree to grow through it. The vertical trunk with its speckled white bark contrasts nicely with the horizontal planes of the floor, trellis, and garage siding.

The paved, trellis-covered space is used almost entirely for dining and is distinctly separate from the grass-floored portion of the garden, where a chaise longue and comfortable chairs clustered under the apple tree are inviting even on the hottest days.

Turn-of-the-Century Twist
· 50′ × 70′· Figure 75 ·

This sturdy house may seem far from architecturally pleasing from without, but like so many houses of its period it has spacious, comfortable rooms that lend themselves to modern treatment. In this case, the structure of the house inspires an enclosed garden that is an obvious extension of indoor space. It looks pleasant from indoors at all times of the year and is easily large enough

to seat a dozen to fifteen people. It is bounded by the house, a garage wall, the parking area, a rear alley, and a 6-foot sapling fence belonging to the neighbor on the south.

The two windows in the dining room's rear wall are replaced with insulated sliding glass doors (Figure 76), which allow early-morning sunlight into the house and

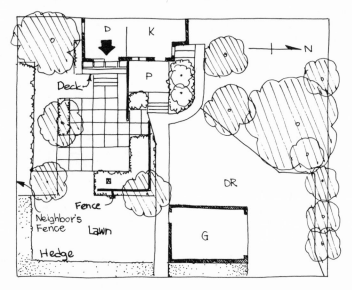

Figure 75

make the indoor space seem larger. A wooden deck at floor level, from which three steps lead down to the floor of the garden, extends four feet beyond the house. A wisteria trellis above the deck connects the garden to the house and camouflages the mass of the second story when viewed from within the garden. The trellis also shades the glass doors from late-morning summer sun.

Figure 76

The garden floor is a grid of 4-foot concrete squares. A strip of bamboolike reed fencing conceals the south side of the service porch, and an L-shaped extension screens the garage, turncourt, and service walk. The fence also provides privacy within the garden and the dining room. Notice that the two fence sections are not connected but rather overlap to cut the view to the kitchen steps while permitting free access at all times. The reed fencing repeats the vertical texture of the already existing split-sapling fence along the south boundary. The privet hedge along the alley is refurbished and pruned into a formal hedge and extended around the corner to overlap with the sapling fence. This repeats the L-shape of the reed fencing and provides a dense protective screen from the traffic in the alley.

The planting beds, locked into the paving pattern, contain evergreen carpets of vinca. A small piece of sculpture in front of the reed fence can be seen and enjoyed from indoors and out. A wisp of vine on the fence softens the geometry of the whole. The planting beds against the south fence contain spring bulbs, daylilies, plantain lily (*Hosta*), ferns, and other shade-tolerant plants. Three dogwoods provide additional interest and autumn color. One is placed on the alley side of the reed fence to screen the view of the garage

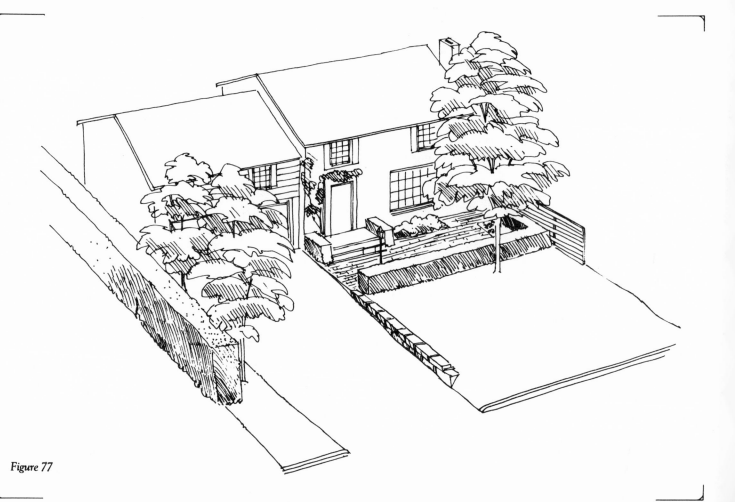

Figure 77

from within the house, but the limbs hanging over the fence can still be enjoyed from indoors. The view of the service porch is partially concealed by lilacs.

This small and simple garden is interesting because of the tightly organized pattern. The grass panels act as outdoor rugs, level with the paving and easily mowed, which add to the roomlike quality of the space.

A half-dozen circular and free-form chairs and two or three small, round, and low tables are used to furnish the garden. These shapes soften the geometry of the grid and look good wherever they are placed. Square or rectangular furniture, on the other hand, must be carefully arranged to conform to the patterns of the garden.

Entry Plaza
· *Figure 77* ·

Awkwardly proportioned houses often appear particularly uninviting. This two-story dark-red brick house 8 or 10 feet above street level has an adjoining garage that was originally covered with shingles painted white. Since the masses of the two parts are nearly equal, they appeared to be two unrelated buildings.

Painting the two parts one color unifies structure.

Tall sheared evergreen sentinels are removed and the steep steps are enlarged to the full width of the entry platform to deemphasize the vertical dimensions of the house. The extra-wide steps accentuate the horizontal dimensions of the platform and are spacious and convenient. In addition, a large area at ground level is converted to a brick entrance court or plaza enclosed by a waist-high evergreen hedge that transforms it into an outdoor entrance hall. The existing tree, as it grows larger and provides more of a canopy over the court, adds to this effect while diminishing the apparent height of the house.

This dooryard garden is entirely structural and functional, and it needs little care or horticultural ability. The entry court also improves the view from the living-room picture window. On the house side of the hedge, along the edge of the brick paving, space is left to plant groundcover or small flowering shrubs or plants.

Narrow and Deep Lot
· *50′ × 80′* · *Figure 78* ·

In recent years many older houses in and around cities have been extensively remodeled, proving conclusively

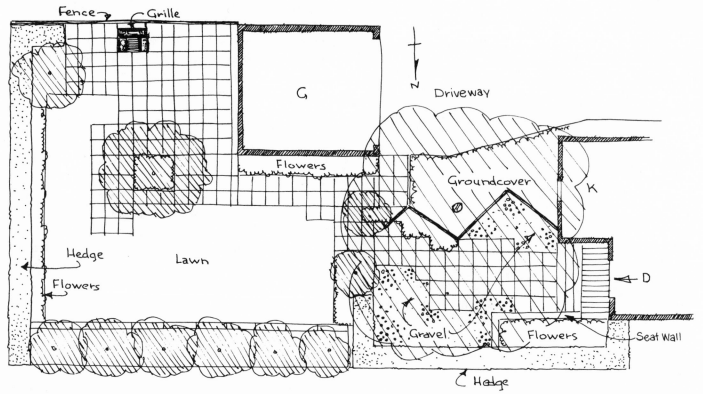

Figure 78

Fence → ⌐Grille

G

Driveway

N

Groundcover

K

Flowers

⌀

Hedge

D

Lawn

Flowers

Gravel

Flowers

Seat Wall

Hedge

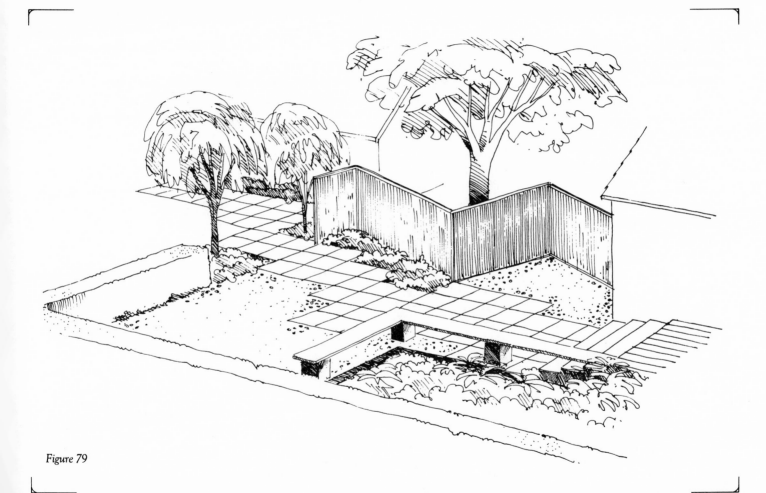

Figure 79

that moving to the suburbs is not the only way to improve one's environment. This house, built around 1910 on a lot 50 feet wide (almost a third of which is devoured by the driveway), is typical of many houses of that period.

A door opening from the kitchen onto the driveway a few steps below allowed only indirect access to the backyard. Replacing the dining-room windows with glass doors leading directly to the garden affords additional access to the backyard (Figure 79). Because the first floor is above garden level, a small wooden deck and broad stairs offer the necessary transition between levels. A wooden seat wall on one side of the paving extends the wood structure. A large oak tree forms a canopy over this portion of the garden, and an evergreen hedge gives enclosure on the left side. A zigzag bamboo screen separates the garden from the driveway and also shortens the long, linear direction of so narrow a space. The garden floor is covered with an evergreen carpet of ivy and 2-by-2-foot precast paving blocks, all of which creates a slightly oriental mood.

The space closest to the house serves as an entryway to the more open garden space beyond and provides adequate seating for a small group of people. The generous paved area behind the garage flows smoothly into a flat lawn panel. This is where family and friends gather in larger groups, their privacy ensured by the enclosing fence, hedge, and row of tall shrubs. Two small flowering trees furnish shade.

The grid—here in a 2-foot module—interlocks the lawn and paving, yet allows an almost wandering route between the open garden and the house.

Welcome Yard
· *Figure 80* ·

Front yards might also be called "welcome yards," since they lead people to the front door. This 1920s house on a large lot with big trees was remodeled to foster such a welcome. Originally, entry was gained through a dark, glass-enclosed porch. Stripping the glass and bringing the entrance around from the left side to the front of the porch creates a wide and generous approach. A stone retaining wall constructed parallel to the front of the house counteracts the change in level near the base of the new porch stairs as well as the downward slope of the land to the north. A 2½-foot evergreen hedge on top of the wall conceals the secondary walkway to the side porch and helps unify the chimney, dormers, and other

Figure 80

vertical lines on the house facade. Painting the house one color reduces the complexity of the facade; the brick of the porch floor, stairs, and paved apron simulate a red carpet rolled from the front door to the parking area. This also dramatizes the effect of the deeply recessed entrance door.

The terrace floor between the walk and the house is carpeted with evergreen groundcover. Large pots of flowering and foliage plants are used in groups on the steps to provide color in spring, summer, and fall. A few small dogwoods are planted close to the house. Since there are many trees on the property, the dogwoods lock the terrace and house into the remainder of the landscape. The existing multistemmed maple at the right end of the wall is incorporated into the scheme by extending the retaining wall around it.

This is another example of the rebirth of an older property by applying straightforward design principles that cater to modern needs.

Flower-Filled Backyard
· 55′ × 60′ · Figure 81 ·

Many small backyards look even smaller because of the large amount of space devoted to turncourts for au-

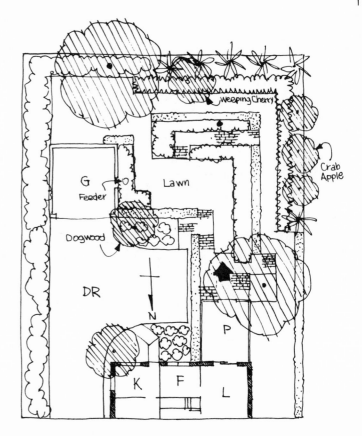

Figure 81

tomobiles, especially when a confining screen is placed between the living space and the turncourt. Making the garden portion of the backyard so attractive that it draws attention away from the asphalt may be the best way to prevent this. Keeping the cars out of sight in the garage is another solution.

The garden in Figures 81 and 82 is bounded by the house and screened porch on the north, the turncourt and garage on the east, a well-established border of pines at the rear, and flowering crab-apple trees on the west. A very old pink dogwood stands at the front corner of the garage, an oak is near the back corner, a medium-large elm is located by the corner of the porch, and an old weeping Japanese cherry tree constitutes part of the rear border.

A door installed at the rear of the porch provides direct access to the garden (and allows for the removal of the side door opening onto the turncourt). The lead statue and shell-shaped birdbath are placed on an axis that bisects both the porch and the living room and provides a focal point around which soft masses of flowering plants are gathered. Low hedges of convex-leaf Japanese holly act as a backdrop for the flower beds. Even when the garden is covered with snow, the hedge remains definitive and accentuates the lead sculpture.

Additional holly hedges separate the garden from the turncourt and confine attention to the garden.

The brick paving close to the porch measures only 12 feet by 13 feet, yet works to hold the garden design together. On one side it functions as a walk, allowing access to the turncourt, and on the other side it edges the flower bed, locking it into the overall scheme. The bricks are butted side by side, on edge, the length of a brick establishing the width of the edging.

The brick wall bisecting the rear bed permits easy access within the bed, but does not reduce the colorful effect of the mass of flowers. Even when the grass is wet, it is possible to weed, plant, and clip within the flower beds from a position on the walk. The path is also an inviting walkway that appears longer than it actually is.

Roses, a particular favorite of this gardener, are planted against the house and near the old dogwood, really outside the main garden. Nonetheless, they can be seen and enjoyed from within, because the dividing hedges are only two feet tall—still tall enough to block out some of the turncourt.

A white azalea and pink dogwood that bloom simultaneously emerge from an evergreen groundcover against the garage wall. A weathered feeder is placed close to the garage window, and a gray matchstick blind (the same color as the exterior shutters) is hung inside the window to obstruct vision into the garage.

Creamy yellow daylilies planted in a single row along the edge of the turf path, where they had previously grown in irregular groups, form an **L**-shaped hedge in front of the crab-apple-and-pine border. In the spring, the weeping cherry tree arches some of its limbs over the rear of the path, forming a fragile tunnel of pink flowers.

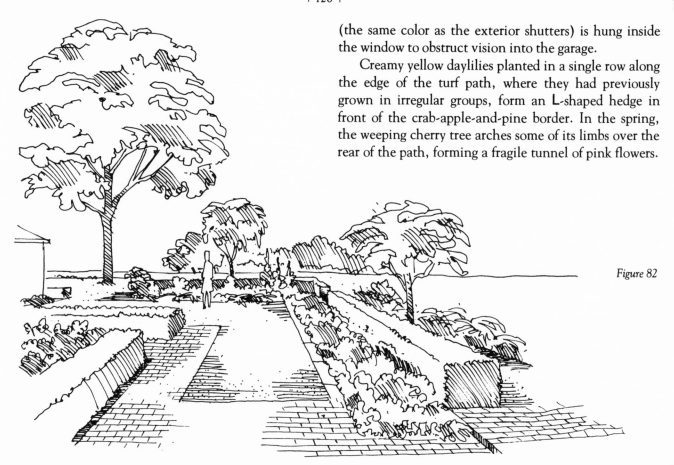

Figure 82

Daffodils are planted in clusters behind the daylily hedge so that the growing daylily leaves hide the daffodil foliage as it begins to yellow.

Clusters of pink, silvery lavender, and deep plum-colored tulips bloom simultaneously with the Japanese weeping cherry tree just as the creamy white pansies and perennials are beginning to grow. Pink dianthus, sweet William, astilbe, phlox, purple and fragrant lavender, and blue delphiniums provide rich color through June. Petunias thrive until the first frost, and chrysanthemums carry the garden well into the fall. Whenever the beds become too much work, an evergreen groundcover such as vinca, fine in texture and neat in appearance, can be planted. Thus this garden can grow into a spectator garden to be viewed from the porch, requiring minimum maintenance.

Front-Yard Meadow
· Figure 83 ·

The trunks of four old trees on this large and otherwise treeless meadow contrast with the low, horizontal house and anchor the house within the lot, so any landscaping should do little more than emphasize the trees and create an entranceway to the house. The door is to the left of the large window wall and provides an awkward view into the living room for anyone approaching the house, particularly by way of the narrow, L-shaped porch. The new dooryard lures attention away from the window while at the same time creating a more generous and welcoming entranceway. From within the living room the dooryard provides an interesting vista and separation from the meadow, but since anyone standing in the living room can look over the edge to the meadow, the dooryard is not confining.

The line of the dwarf winged euonymus hedge was determined by the relationship of the grove of trees to the desired direction of foot traffic. It also avoids, in its zigzag line, interference with the septic tank and its drainage field. Euonymus is of oriental origin, but it seems very much at home in our native landscapes. In some regions it holds its leaves well into winter. Its dense twig structure remains distinctive throughout the winter and is especially attractive with snow on it. In fall, its brilliant rose, crimson, and bronzy red foliage blends well with the dark crimson leaves and ornamental red berries of the dogwoods, and it contrasts just as favorably with the yellows, golds, and warm browns of the larger trees. A full-sized winged euonymus on the north side of the driveway bears the same color and texture as the hedge but retains its natural form.

A needle-type evergreen, such as Japanese yew, can be used for the hedge, although yew hedges tend to be more formal and less suited to country gardens than deciduous hedges. The lack of evergreen in the euonymous hedge is compensated for by evergreen groundcovers and shaggy dwarf yews within the dooryard. The bed against the inside of the hedge is almost entirely devoted to flowering plants.

Seven dogwoods further enclose the entrance garden. The smaller trees close to the house reduce the dwarfing effect of the large trees. Four of the dogwoods provide a low-branched screen at the hedge's terminus at the southeast corner of the house.

A large tree planted southeast of the entranceway, just across the hedge from the flower bed, blocks out late-morning summer sun. The rest of the front yard is meadowlike turf, although the lawn area within the hedge is mowed as close as an ordinary lawn.

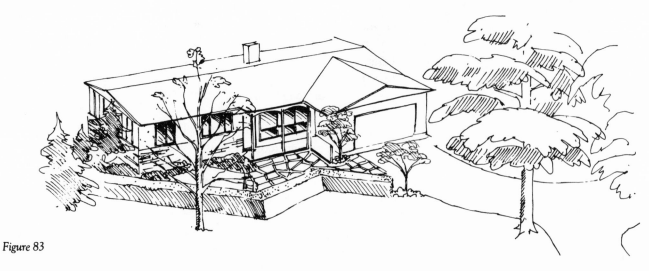

Figure 83

The paving, made of large chunks of natural stone, is well suited to an informal country setting. The stones rest on a sand base, with tufts of moss, mother-of-thyme, and other plants growing between them. It is unwise to use salt or other de-icing compounds on the stones, because that might damage the small plants and tree roots. Use sand instead.

Woodland Retreat
• 90' × 140' • Figure 84 •

Overexposure to the sun is no problem with this woodland plot, because the rear portion of the property is scattered with forty or fifty young beech, oak, sassafras, and maple trees. This is an easy-to-care-for outdoor space that abounds with wildflowers in spring, is cool and enjoyable in summer, bright with color in autumn, and sheltered enough to attract many birds in winter (with the help of a well-stocked feeder).

The 3-by-8-foot sliding glass panels at the rear of the dining room make the garden easily accessible to family and guests. As soon as someone enters the front door of the house, he or she is treated to a view of the garden, which makes a small and quite ordinary house exciting to live in and visit. The bay-windowed breakfast nook and kitchen are also exposed to the garden. A rear door in the attached garage provides easy access to storage space for garden furniture and tools.

The builder had left a terrace of earth close to the house, its bank paralleling the rear wall. Because the owners wanted the backyard to remain as close to its natural woodsy state as possible, the bulldozed terrace of earth was modified to allow for paving in a manner which would emphasize the woods.

The lower-level lawn panel (Figure 85) and the paved terrace near the house (Figure 86) help define the garden and bring the woods into focus. Since trees are immovable objects, the shape of the lawn is determined by the position of the trees. Once the lawn panel is established, the gap between the tree opposite the rear garage door and the cluster of trees outside the dining-room window becomes the natural place for access between the terrace and the lawn. The trees separate these spaces, and their trunks and overhanging limbs form a natural arbor between them.

Moving a small amount of soil from behind the garage to where the steps are to be built adequately extends the terrace and gives it a definite shape. In situations such as this, too often the terrace becomes practically

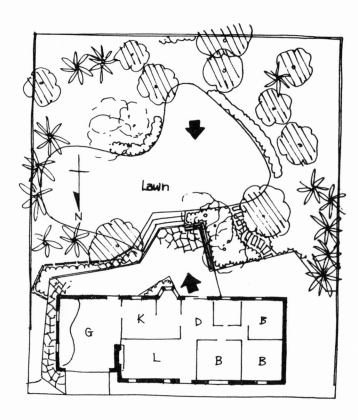

Figure 84

shapeless in an attempt to make it more "naturalistic," rather than admitting that it is man-made. Since natural vegetation is abundant, here the architectural shape balances the house and the woods, although irregularly placed pieces of dark-gray flagstone help to soften the impact of the terrace.

The planting under the breakfast-room windows breaks what would otherwise be a monotonous junction of paving and house wall and provides a link between the house and the landscape—almost as though the woods have come up through the terrace floor. This overlapping and interlocking of parts of the garden scheme are essential to making each element seem part of the whole.

The paving stones are set without mortar in a bed of sand, but the steps are wood. The wooden steps allow free circulation of air beneath them, while remaining informal and completely suited to a woodsy situation. Because of modern lumber preservatives, many kinds of wood—not just the typical redwood or cypress—can be used in gardens.

The seat is made of 2-by-6-inch planks—three strips cleated side by side to make it 18 inches wide—using flue tiles as supports, cut so that the finished seat is approximately 15 inches high. This creates a pleasing design that relates to the shape of the terrace, is comfortable for sitting, handy for holding picnic trays, and wide enough for stretching out on to contemplate the moon and the stars. It also acts as a railing, preventing anyone from stepping off the high side of the terrace.

The lower turf panel is edged with low-growing plants, which look as if they grow there naturally. Tumbling euonymus vines, climbing hydrangea, oak-leaf hydrangea, fragrant sumac, and common daylilies grow thickly enough to form a barrier between the lawn and the woods, except where paths leading into the woods are visible. These are edged by violets, daffodils, crocuses, grape hyacinths, ferns, and wildflowers.

Hemlocks, at home in the woods, are planted to provide privacy where views from neighboring properties

Figure 85

Figure 86

are most penetrating. These are especially beautiful in the winter. An inexpensive wire fence covered with various kinds of vines—bittersweet, woodbine, euonymus, trumpet creeper—further encloses the garden and prevents children from running across the property and trampling the wildflowers growing in the woods.

Afterword

Building a garden—from the paper-planning stage to the first moment you relax in the shade of a tree you've planted—is a stimulating and rewarding adventure. Few of us today have the opportunity to be craftsmen—to act, and to see the direct results of our action. While building an automobile, computer, or skyscraper may be beyond our capabilities, building a garden is not. We are, after all, biological creatures, more related to the out-of-doors than to the computer and skyscraper, and gardens give us the chance to develop our intuitive eye.

Birth, growth, old age, death—these are phases of the garden no less than of human life, not only in terms of individual trees, shrubs, and other plants, but also in terms of overall composition. We are apt to be overwhelmed by the gardens of the past—Villa Lante, Versailles, Hampton Court—but then we must remind ourselves that these, too, were once young; they have gone through many changes over the years. A garden is never static. Even within the very short span of a year, it affords us countless opportunities for change.

James Rose, landscape architect, put it simply: "A garden is an experience."

Appendix • Trees, Shrubs, Climbing Plants, and Groundcovers for Landscaping

The plants in this appendix are grouped into six lists according to size, the most important factor in determining how they are used in shaping landscape spaces. Other pertinent factors are charted, but these are mere indicators, so additional reading is strongly recommended. (Probably the best general books on the subject are *Trees for American Gardens* and *Shrubs and Vines for American Gardens*, both by Donald Wyman, Macmillan, 1971, 1973.) It is also a good idea to visit botanical and other public gardens, arboreta, and parks, where you can observe a variety of trees and shrubs in various stages of maturity. There are many special characteristics impossible to express here; you should experience them.

The author's prejudices enter into some of the choices, but as the result, I would like to believe, of knowledge and experience. It is also impossible to include everything. Certain very large, slow-growing, but nevertheless desirable plants—American and European beeches, white oak, etc.—have been excluded because, if you're going out to buy a tree, it is presumed that you want fairly quick results. On the other hand, some very fast-growing trees—silver maple, ailanthus—have not been included because they are relatively weak-wooded.

This list includes only woody plants. There are many herbaceous perennial plants also extremely useful in shaping landscape (for these one can refer to *Low Maintenance Perennials*, by Robert S. Hebb, Quadrangle Press, 1975).

Explanation of terms used in the charts:

evergreen • remains green year-round; either broad-leaf or needle-leaved

deciduous • loses leaves in winter

autumn color · distinctive foliage color in autumn

flowers · conspicuous flowering habit*

fragrance · obvious fragrance in flowers, foliage, and/or twigs

ornamental fruit · colorful berries or berrylike fruits in autumn

interesting bark · texture, color, gloss, etc.

distinctive form · unique overall character in growth habit

group well · several plants of the same kind can be used in informal or formal groupings set rather close together to form shady groves or dense screens

specimen · good-looking enough to stand alone

dense mass · as in shrubs, impenetrable mass of branches, twigs; good screen plants

sheared hedge · can be maintained as formal hedge

natural hedge · can be left unsheared or only lightly clipped to form softer, informal hedge

*The label "flowers" on landscape plans in this book refers to annuals, herbaceous perennials, bulbs, etc.

hedgerow · trees and large shrubs which will make informal hedgerow, unpruned

climbing plant · will climb on fences, walls, etc.— may need support

carpetlike cover · will cover ground in dense carpet

irregular cover · irregular in texture, height

grows on fences, trellises · climbing plants that will twine or otherwise support themselves on poles, wires, trellises, etc.

grows on walls · climbing plants that will hold fast to wood, stone, or masonry walls without other support

All botanical names are according to *Hortus Third* (Macmillan, 1976). If the trade name differs, it follows in parentheses. The term "cultivar" refers to a cultivated variety and is designated in the following lists by single quotes—e.g., *Acer platanoides* 'Schwedleri'. Cultivars can also be expressed with the abbreviation cv.—in the previous example, *Acer platanoides* cv. Schwedleri—both terminologies are valid. And the symbol × (as in List B for *Aesculus* × *carnea* 'Briotii') indicates a hybrid.

A.   Large Trees

· over 50' ·

These trees are chiefly for shade and will eventually tower above the house, but they take many years to reach mature height. Purchase them as large as possible, but remember, they don't have to be fifty or a hundred years old to provide a great deal of shade and pleasurable cover for the yard.

evergreen	deciduous	autumn color	flowers	fragrance	ornamental fruit	interesting bark	distinctive form	group well	specimen	COMMON NAME	BOTANICAL NAME
•							•		•	White Fir	*Abies concolor*
•				•					•	Fraser Fir	*Abies fraseri*
•							•		•	Nikko Fir	*Abies homolepis*
	•								•	Norway Maple	*Acer platanoides*
	•								•	Schwedler Maple	*Acer platanoides 'Schwedleri'*
	•	•			•			•	•	Red or Swamp Maple	*Acer rubrum*
	•	•			•			•	•	October Glory Maple	*Acer rubrum 'October Glory'*
	•	•			•		•	•	•	Sugar Maple	*Acer saccharum*

evergreen	deciduous	autumn color	flowers	fragrance	ornamental fruit	interesting bark	distinctive form	group well	specimen	COMMON NAME	BOTANICAL NAME
	•	•			•	•	•		•	Green Mountain Sugar Maple	*Acer saccharum* 'Green Mountain'
	•	•	•				•		•	Common or European Horsechestnut	*Aesculus hippocastanum*
	•	•					•		•	Katsura Tree	*Cercidiphyllum japonicum*
	•	•				•	•		•	Rosehill Ash	*Fraxinus americana* 'Rosehill'
	•	•					•			Marshall's Seedless Ash	*Fraxinus pennsylvanica lanceolata* 'Marshall's Seedless'
	•	•				•	•			Maidenhair Tree (male only)	*Ginkgo biloba*
	•	•		•	•	•	•	•	•	Sweet Gum	*Liquidambar styraciflua*
•							•		•	Serbian Spruce	*Picea omorika*
•						•	•		•	Lace-bark Pine	*Pinus bungeana*
•						•	•	•	•	Austrian Pine	*Pinus nigra*
•				•			•	•	•	White Pine	*Pinus strobus*
	•						•			Bolleana Poplar	*Populus alba* 'Bolleana'
•							•	•		Douglas Fir	*Pseudotsuga menziesii (P. taxifolia)*
	•	•							•	Northern Red Oak	*Quercus rubra (Q. borealis)*

evergreen	deciduous	autumn color	flowers	fragrance	ornamental fruit	interesting bark	distinctive form	group well	specimen	COMMON NAME	BOTANICAL NAME
	•		•	•		•		•	•	American Linden	*Tilia americana*
	•		•	•			•	•	•	Small-leaved European Linden	*Tilia cordata*
	•		•	•			•		•	Silver Linden	*Tilia tomentosa*
•							•	•		Canada Hemlock	*Tsuga canadensis*
•							•	•		Carolina Hemlock	*Tsuga caroliniana*

B. Medium Trees
· 30′–50′ ·

These trees are not so large in old age as the first group, but are still interesting and useful. While some eventually may reach more than 50′, they are valuable landscape trees.

evergreen	deciduous	autumn color	flowers	fragrance	ornamental fruit	dense mass	open form	group well	specimen	COMMON NAME	BOTANICAL NAME
	•	•	•					•	•	Red Horse Chestnut	*Aesculus × carnea* 'Briotii'
	•	•	•	•	•			•	•	Allegheny Shadbush or Sarvisberry	*Amelanchier laevis*
	•	•			•			•	•	Paper or Canoe Birch	*Betula papyrifera*
	•	•			•		•	•	•	European White Birch	*Betula pendula*
	•	•			•			•	•	European Hornbeam	*Carpinus betulus*
	•	•	•	•	•		•		•	Yellowwood	*Cladrastis lutea*
	•					•	•		•	Shademaster Thornless Honey Locust	*Gleditsia triacanthos inermis* 'Shademaster'
	•				•		•		•	Kentucky Coffee Tree	*Gymnocladus dioica*

evergreen	deciduous	autumn color	flowers	fragrance	ornamental fruit	dense mass	open form	group well	specimen	COMMON NAME	BOTANICAL NAME
•					•		•		•	American Holly (includes many cultivars, such as Amy, Cardinal, Merry Xmas, Old Heavy Berry, etc.)	*Ilex opaca*
	•	•	•		•		•		•	Siberian Crab (includes several cultivars)	*Malus baccata*
	•	•			•		•		•	Sour Gum, Tupelo, Pepperidge	*Nyssa sylvatica*
	•	•	•		•		•		•	Sargent Cherry	*Prunus sargentii*
	•		•		•		•		•	Yoshino or Potomac Cherry	*Prunus yedoensis*
	•			•	•		•		•	Babylon Weeping Willow	*Salix babylonica*
	•	•							•	Japanese Pagoda Tree, Chinese Scholar Tree	*Sophora japonica*
	•	•	•	•	•				•	Korean Mountain Ash	*Sorbus alnifolia*
	•	•				•			•	Japanese Zelkova	*Zelkova serrata*

C. Small Trees

· 15′–30′ ·

Some of the most beautiful of garden plants belong to this group. They are extremely useful in both small gardens and large. Some can be allowed to develop branches low to the ground and thereby serve to screen out unwanted views or to gain privacy. With lower limbs cut off, some of these same trees create small pools of shade, and in groups they make wonderful leafy groves for larger areas or longer walkways.

evergreen	deciduous	autumn color	flowers	fragrance	ornamental fruit	dense mass	open form	group well	specimen	hedgerow	COMMON NAME	BOTANICAL NAME
	•					•				•	Hedge Maple	*Acer campestre*
	•		•			•	•			•	Amur Maple	*Acer ginnala*
	•			•		•	•				Paperback Maple	*Acer griseum*
	•			•	•	•	•	•		•	Japanese Maple (includes many cultivars)	*Acer palmatum*
	•			•			•	•	•		Silk Tree, Mimosa	*Albizia julibrissin*
	•	•		•	•		•	•		•	Shadberry, Juneberry	*Amelanchier canadensis*

evergreen	deciduous	autumn color	flowers	fragrance	ornamental fruit	dense mass	open form	group well	specimen	hedgerow	COMMON NAME	BOTANICAL NAME
	•	•	•		•	•	•	•	•	•	Pink Shadblow	*Amelanchier canadensis* 'Robin Hill pink'
	•	•	•		•	•	•	•	•	•	American Redbud	*Cercis canadensis*
•						•	•			•	Plume Sawara Cypress	*Chamaecyparis pisifera* 'Plumosa'
	•	•	•				•	•	•	•	Flowering Dogwood	*Cornus florida*
	•	•	•				•	•	•	•	Cloud 9 Dogwood	*Cornus florida* 'Cloud 9'
	•	•	•				•	•	•	•	Pink Flowering Dogwood	*Cornus florida* 'Rubra'
	•	•	•				•	•	•	•	Super Red Dogwood	*Cornus florida* 'Super Red'
	•	•	•		•		•	•	•	•	Kousa Dogwood	*Cornus kousa*
	•	•	•				•	•		•	Cornelian Cherry	*Cornus mas*
	•	•	•					•	•		Smoke Tree	*Cotinus coggygria*
	•	•	•		•		•	•	•	•	Cockspur Thorn	*Crataegus crus-galli*
	•		•		•	•	•	•		•	English Hawthorn	*Crataegus laevigata (C. oxyacantha)*
	•		•		•	•	•	•		•	Lavalle Hawthorn	*Crataegus × lavallei*
	•					•	•			•	Russian Olive	*Elaeagnus angustifolia*

evergreen	deciduous	autumn color	flowers	fragrance	ornamental fruit	dense mass	open form	group well	specimen	hedgerow	COMMON NAME	BOTANICAL NAME
	•	•	•			•	•		•		Franklinia	*Franklinia alatamaha*
	•	•	•			•		•	•		Carolina Silver-bell	*Halesia carolina*
	•		•					•			Varnish Tree, Golden-rain Tree	*Koelreuteria paniculata*
	•		•	•		•			•		Golden-chain	*Laburnum × watereri (L. vossii)*
	•		•	•		•			•		Merrill Magnolia	*Magnolia × loebneri* 'Merrill'
	•		•	•	•	•	•		•		Saucer Magnolia	*Magnolia × soulangiana*
•	•	•	•			•	•	•	•	•	Sweet Bay	*Magnolia virginiana*
	•	•	•	•	•		•	•	•		Bob White Flowering Crab Apple	*Malus* 'Bob White'
	•	•	•	•	•		•	•	•		Showy Crab Apple	*Malus floribunda*
	•	•	•	•	•		•	•	•		Katherine Flowering Apple	*Malus* 'Katherine'
	•		•	•	•		•	•	•		Van Eseltine Flowering Crab Apple	*Malus spectabilis* 'Van Eseltine'
	•	•		•	•	•	•	•			American Hop Hornbeam	*Ostrya virginiana*
	•	•	•		•		•	•	•		Sourwood	*Oxydendrum arboreum*
	•	•				•	•				Amur Cork Tree	*Phellodendron amurense*

evergreen	deciduous	autumn color	flowers	fragrance	ornamental fruit	dense mass	open form	group well	specimen	hedgerow	COMMON NAME	BOTANICAL NAME
•						•			•		Swiss Stone Pine	*Pinus cembra*
•					•	•	•		•		Tanyosho or Japanese Umbrella Pine	*Pinus densiflora* 'Umbraculifer'
	•	•			•				•		Autumn Flowering Cherry	*Prunus subhirtella* 'Autumnalis'
	•	•			•	•			•		Weeping Japanese Cherry	*Prunus subhirtella* 'Pendula'
	•	•	•		•	•	•		•	•	Callery or Bradford Pear	*Pyrus calleryana*
	•	•	•		•				•		European MountainAsh	*Sorbus aucuparia*
	•	•			•	•	•		•		Japanese Stewartia	*Stewartia pseudocamellia*
	•			•	•	•	•		•	•	Japanese Tree Lilac	*Syringa reticulata (S. amurensis japonica)*

D. Large Shrubs
· 6'–12' ·

The distinction between tree and shrub is sometimes arbitrary. Shrubs usually have more than one stem or trunk arising from the ground, trees only one. Yet some shrubs (common lilac, for example) can be pruned to one or two trunks to become treelike. And some trees (Japanese maple, Sargent crab apple) are so dense and low-growing that they form a shrublike mass. It is growth habit that determines usage, so some plants that might be found in tree lists elsewhere are here considered shrubs. Many of these are the most spectacular of flowering plants. Others are sturdy, quiet evergreens. Because most are over 6 feet, they are useful as screens and hedges.

evergreen	deciduous	autumn color	flowers	fragrance	ornamental fruit	dense mass	open form	group well	specimen	sheared hedge	natural hedge	hedgerow	COMMON NAME	BOTANICAL NAME
	•	•	•				•	•					Bottlebush Buckeye	*Aesculus parviflora*
	•	•	•				•				•		Red Chokeberry	*Aronia arbutifolia*
	•	•	•			•	•						Chinese Redbud	*Cercis chinensis*
	•	•	•	•	•		•		•	•			Flowering Quince (includes several cultivars)	*Chaenomeles speciosa* (*C. lagenaria*)

evergreen	deciduous	autumn color	flowers	fragrance	ornamental fruit	dense mass	open form	group well	specimen	sheared hedge	natural hedge	hedgerow	COMMON NAME	BOTANICAL NAME
	•	•	•	•		•	•				•		Fringe Tree	*Chionanthus virginicus*
	•	•	•	•	•		•	•			•		Washington Thorn	*Crataegus phaenopyrum*
	•		•	•	•	•	•	•		•	•		Autumn Elaeagnus	*Elaeagnus umbellata*
	•	•	•			•		•		•	•		Red-vein Enkianthus	*Enkianthus campanulatus*
	•				•		•		•	•			Winged Euonymus	*Euonymus alata*
•				•	•		•				•		Spreading Euonymus	*Euonymus kiautschovica* (E. patens)
	•		•			•		•				•	Showy Border Forsythia (includes many cultivars, such as Linwood Gold, Spring Gold Primulina)	*Forsythia × intermedia* 'Spectabilis'
	•	•	•	•			•		•				Arnold Witch Hazel	*Hamamelis × intermedia* 'Arnold Promise'
	•	•	•	•			•	•	•				Chinese Witch Hazel	*Hamamelis mollis*
	•	•	•	•			•	•	•		•		Vernal Witch Hazel	*Hamamelis vernalis*
	•	•			•			•			•		Black Alder, Winterberry	*Ilex verticillata*
•			•			•	•	•			•		Mountain Laurel	*Kalmia latifolia*

evergreen	deciduous	autumn color	flowers	fragrance	ornamental fruit	dense mass	open form	group well	specimen	sheared hedge	natural hedge	hedgerow	COMMON NAME	BOTANICAL NAME
	•				•					•	•		Amur Privet	*Ligustrum amurense*
	•				•			•		•	•		Ibolium Privet	*Ligustrum × ibolium*
	•				•				•				California Privet	*Ligustrum ovalifolium*
	•	•	•	•		•	•						Spicebush	*Lindera benzoin*
	•		•	•	•				•				Star Magnolia	*Magnolia stellata*
•		•		•	•		•	•					Leather-leaf Mahonia	*Mahonia bealei*
	•	•	•	•	•		•				•		Arnold Crab Apple	*Malus × arnoldiana*
	•	•	•	•	•		•			•	•		Sargent Crab Apple	*Malus sargentii*
•	•		•		•		•		•	•			Laland Fire Thorn (includes many cultivars)	*Pyracantha coccinea* 'Lalandei'
	•	•			•		•			•	•		Tallhedge Buckthorn	*Rhamnus frangula* 'Columnaris'
	•	•	•	•	•		•	•		•			Flame Azalea	*Rhododendron calendulaceum*
•		•	•	•	•		•	•		•			Catawba Rhododendron (includes many cultivars, such as Charles Dickens, Everestianum, Roseum Elegans, also several Dexter Hybrids)	*Rhododendron catawbiense*

evergreen	deciduous	autumn color	flowers	fragrance	ornamental fruit	dense mass	open form	group well	specimen	sheared hedge	natural hedge	hedgerow	COMMON NAME	BOTANICAL NAME
	•	•	•		•		•	•					Ghent Hybrid Azaleas (includes many cultivars, such as Daviesii, Nancy Waterer, Pallas, Narcissi-flora, etc.)	*Rhododendron × gandavense*
	•						•	•		•			Torch Azalea	*Rhododendron kaempferi*
	•	•	•				•	•					Korean Rhododendron (also cv. Cornell Pink)	*Rhododendron mucronulatum*
	•	•	•				•	•		•			Royal Azalea	*Rhododendron schlippenbachii*
	•	•	•	•			•	•		•			Pink-shell Azalea	*Rhododendron vaseyi*
	•	•			•	•	•	•			•	•	Shining Sumac	*Rhus copallina*
	•	•		•	•	•	•	•			•	•	Staghorn Sumac	*Rhus typhina*
	•	•	•		•		•			•			Father Hugo Rose	*Rosa hugonis*
	•	•	•			•				•			Bridalwreath	*Spiraea prunifolia*
	•		•				•		•				Japanese Snowbell	*Styrax japonica*
	•		•	•		•				•	•		Chinese Lilac	*Syringa × chinensis*
	•	•	•	•		•	•			•	•		Common Lilac (includes many cultivars)	*Syringa vulgaris*

evergreen	deciduous	autumn color	flowers	fragrance	ornamental fruit	dense mass	open form	group well	specimen	sheared hedge	natural hedge	hedgerow	COMMON NAME	BOTANICAL NAME
•					•		•		•				Upright Japanese Yew	*Taxus cuspidata* 'Capitata'
•					•		•		•	•			Dense Yew	*Taxus cuspidata* 'Densiformis'
•					•		•		•	•			Hatfield Yew	*Taxus × media* 'Hatfieldii'
•					•	•		•					Sargent Weeping Hemlock	*Tsuga canadensis* 'Pendula'
	•	•	•	•	•	•					•		Burkwood Viburnum Fragrant Snowball	*Viburnum × burkwoodii*
	•	•	•		•		•	•			•		Japanese Snowball	*Viburnum plicatum*
	•	•	•		•		•	•			•		Doublefile Viburnum	*Viburnum plicatum tomentosum*
•		•			•		•	•					Leather-leaf Viburnum	*Viburnum rhytidophyllum*
	•	•	•		•		•	•			•		Tea Viburnum	*Viburnum setigerum (V. theiferum)*
	•	•	•		•	•		•			•	•	Siebold Viburnum	*Viburnum sieboldii*

E. Small Shrubs

· under 6′ ·

Here are several plants particularly valued for foliage, overall form, and texture. Many are "accent plants," shrubs that attract more than quiet attention, in some cases with flamboyant color. Others can be used for low hedges that outline garden space and edgings along walkways.

evergreen	deciduous	autumn color	flowers	fragrance	ornamental fruit	dense mass	distinctive form	group well	specimen	sheared hedge	natural hedge	COMMON NAME	BOTANICAL NAME
•			•		•	•		•		•	•	Wintergreen Barberry	*Berberis julianae*
•		•			•		•			•	•	Mentor Barberry	*Berberis × mentorensis*
	•	•			•	•	•			•	•	Japanese Barberry	*Berberis thunbergii* 'Atropurpurea'
•				•		•	•			•	•	Dwarf Korean Boxwood	*Buxus microphylla koreana*
•				•		•	•			•	•	Common Boxwood (includes several cultivars)	*Buxus sempervirens*
	•	•			•		•			•	•	Lesser Flowering Quince	*Chaenomeles japonica*
•							•		•		•	Dwarf Hinoki Cypress	*Chamaecyparis obtusa* 'Nana'

evergreen	deciduous	autumn color	flowers	fragrance	ornamental fruit	dense mass	distinctive form	group well	specimen	sheared hedge	natural hedge	COMMON NAME	BOTANICAL NAME
	●	●	●	●		●					●	Summer-sweet	*Clethra alnifolia*
	●	●		●	●	●						Cranberry Cotoneaster	*Cotoneaster apiculatus*
	●	●		●	●	●	●					Spreading Cotoneaster	*Cotoneaster divaricatus*
	●	●		●		●		●				Willowleaf Cotoneaster	*Cotoneaster salicifolius*
	●	●				●						Warminster Broom	*Cytisus × praecox*
	●	●			●	●			●	●		Dwarf Winged Euonymus	*Euonymus alata 'Compacta'*
●				●	●	●			●			Bigleaf Wintercreeper, Evergreen Bittersweet	*Euonymus fortunei vegeta*
	●	●					●					Weeping Forsythia	*Forsythia suspensa*
	●	●				●	●	●				Fothergilla	*Fothergilla major*
	●	●	●			●	●	●				Oak-leaf Hydrangea	*Hydrangea quercifolia*
●			●			●			●	●		Japanese Holly (includes several cultivars)	*Ilex crenata*
●					●	●	●				●	Compact Pfitzer Juniper	*Juniperus chinensis 'Pfitzerana Compacta'*
●		●				●	●					Drooping Leucothoe	*Leucothoe fontanesiana (L. catesbaei)*

evergreen	deciduous	autumn color	flowers	fragrance	ornamental fruit	dense mass	distinctive form	group well	specimen	sheared hedge	natural hedge	COMMON NAME	BOTANICAL NAME
	•	•			•		•		•		•	Regel Privet	*Ligustrum obtusifolium regelianum*
•		•		•		•		•				Oregon Holly Grape	*Mahonia aquifolium*
•	•		•	•	•	•	•					Bayberry	*Myrica pensylvanica*
•		•			•	•	•					Japanese Andromeda	*Pieris japonica*
•			•			•	•					Mugho Pine	*Pinus mugo*
•		•	•		•		•				•	Boule de Neige Rhododendron	*Rhododendron* 'Boule de Neige'
•		•			•		•	•			•	Carolina Rhododendron	*Rhododendron carolinianum*
	•	•			•		•				•	Delaware Valley White Azalea	*Rhododendron* 'Delaware Valley White'
•		•			•		•				•	Hinodegiri Azalea	*Rhododendron* × 'Hinodegiri'
	•	•	•		•		•					Fragrant Sumac	*Rhus aromatica*
	•	•	•	•	•		•				•	Rugosa Rose	*Rosa rugosa*
•					•	•	•		•	•	•	Spreading English Yew	*Taxus baccata* 'Repandens'
•					•	•	•		•	•	•	Dwarf Japanese Yew	*Taxus cuspidata* 'Nana'
	•	•	•	•	•		•	•			•	Compact Fragrant Viburnum	*Viburnum carlesii* 'Compactum'

F.   Groundcovers and Climbing Plants

Groundcovers and climbing plants (or vines) are grouped together, since many climbing plants can also be used as groundcovers. In some cases the cover will be close and carpetlike; in others the plants will provide a more irregular pattern or texture as they grow to different extents.

evergreen	deciduous	autumn color	flowers	ornamental fruit	carpetlike cover	irregular cover	grows on fences, trellises	grows on walls	COMMON NAME	BOTANICAL NAME
•	•					•			Five-leaf Akebia	*Akebia quinata*
	•	•				•	•		Trumpet Creeper	*Campsis radicans* (*Bignonia radicans*)
	•		•		•	•			American Bittersweet	*Celastrus scandens*
	•	•				•			Hybrid Clematis (includes many cultivars)	*Clematis*
	•	•				•			Anemone Clematis	*Clematis montana*
	•	•	•			•			Sweet Autumn Clematis	*Clematis paniculata*

evergreen	deciduous	autumn color	flowers	ornamental fruit	carpetlike cover	irregular cover	grows on fences, trellises	grows on walls	COMMON NAME	BOTANICAL NAME
•	•	•	•	•	•	•		•	Cranberry Cotoneaster	*Cotoneaster apiculatus*
	•		•		•				Purple-leaf Wintercreeper	*Euonymus fortunei* 'Colorata'
•		•			•	•		•	Dwarf Wintercreeper	*Euonymus fortunei* 'Minima'
•					•			•	English Ivy	*Hedera helix*
•					•			•	Hardy English Ivy, Baltic Ivy	*Hedera helix* 'Baltica'
	•	•	•			•	•	•	Climbing Hydrangea	*Hydrangea anomala* (*H. petiolaris*)
•					•				Bar Harbor Juniper	*Juniperus horizontalis* 'Bar Harbor'
•					•				Waukegan Juniper	*Juniperus horizontalis* 'Douglasii'
•					•				Andorra Juniper	*Juniperus horizontalis* 'Plumosa'
•					•				Blue Rug Juniper	*Juniperus horizontalis* 'Wiltonii'
•	•		•			•	•		Hall's Japanese Honeysuckle	*Lonicera japonica* 'Halliana'

evergreen	deciduous	autumn color	flowers	ornamental fruit	carpetlike cover	irregular cover	grows on fences, trellises	grows on walls	COMMON NAME	BOTANICAL NAME
•					•				Japanese Spurge	*Pachysandra terminalis*
	•	•				•	•		Virginia Creeper	*Parthenocissus quinquefolia*
	•	•							Dwarf Boston Ivy	*Parthenocissus tricuspidata* 'Lowii'
•		•			•				Paxistima, Pachistima, Pachystima	*Paxistima canbyi*
	•		•	•	•				Memorial Rose	*Rosa wichuraiana*
•			•		•				Periwinkle, Myrtle	*Vinca minor*
	•	•					•		Japanese Wisteria	*Wisteria floribunda* 'Macrobotrys'
	•	•							Chinese (Common) Wisteria	*Wisteria sinensis*

Index

NOTE: Page numbers in italics indicate illustrations.